What Readers Are Saying ...

[In] *Through the Smoke* . . . you [can] see the real, ugly, raw, and relatable moments that Tyler encountered navigating his new "normal." He questioned himself. He doubted himself. He had real moments, and [the reader can] feel every bit of it. . . . It was a powerful story that I certainly could not put down once I started reading! It is impactful, relatable, and inspiring!

— Sarah Cope

Tyler's transformation into a bully is believable . . . the "I'll hurt you before you hurt me". . .! The disappointments and heartache Tyler experienced make his transformation very much relatable. The resolution of the main character's conflict was my favorite part. If only the world understood that one simple act of kindness can change the whole trajectory!

— Tracey Gallyon

Through the Smoke was an enjoyable read. . . . My feelings about the main character, Tyler Miller, changed throughout the book. I was very sympathetic toward him . . . for what he was going through . . . The story flows well . . . [as] told by Tyler himself. It really helps the reader go "through the smoke" with him and feel what he was feeling and understand why he acted the way he did.

— Laura Holbrook

. . . interesting to read a story from the bully's point of view. It was relatable and, when standing in Tyler's shoes, understandable. . . . This story illustrates that life and people cannot be viewed as black and white; no one is all good or all bad.

— Lisa Allen

Through the Smoke will be impactful . . . Kids can relate to the [main] character's situations and the feelings . . . The RAK [theme] gives the reader exposure to good values and reinforces positivity and kindness.

— Christopher Furry

. . . Impactful. . . . will resonate with the hearts of . . . children, and the bullies of the world may find the motivation to rectify the wrongs they have done to others. This book is going to become a must for read-alouds in classrooms everywhere.

— Tiffany Morrison

Through the Smoke

Printed in the United States of America

ISBN 978-1-946425-43-0 – softcover
ISBN 978-1-946425-46-1 - hardcover

Book Design by CSinclaire Write-Design
Cover Art by David Martinez

• BARNSLEY INK •
RALEIGH, NORTH CAROLINA

• Books by Frank Saraco •

Hugo's Dilemma
The Bald and the Beautiful
It Could Have Been Us
The Ninth Street Mystery

The RAK Initiative Trilogy
Life in the Grand Pause
Light in the Shadow
Through the Smoke

Dedicated to my nephews

Anthony and David

*who allow kindness to steer their journey.
Thank you for making the world a better place
by walking in your genius.*

Through the Smoke

a middle-grade novel

FRANK SARACO

• BARNSLEY INK •
RALEIGH, NORTH CAROLINA

THE RAK INITIATIVE TRILOGY

Book 3

FOR NEARLY TEN YEARS of his life, Tyler Miller was your typical well-mannered kid who aimed to please his parents in all he did. He enjoyed school and the friendships he built from kindergarten. But as his family began to unravel, so did his attitude and behavior. Can he justify his actions as self-preservation, or is he becoming a bully? Amid the disappointments and changes in his home life, Tyler is forced to leave the school he's attended since kindergarten and enroll at Fern Creek Elementary during the second semester of his fifth grade year. Life doesn't seem fair to Tyler, but he has found a way to cope. Unfortunately, it is at the expense of others, including a new student named R.J. Can Tyler's trajectory be changed, or will he be lost in a smokescreen of hurt? The odds are not in his favor.

CONTENTS

Summer Before Fifth Grade, Early August

EVEN THE BEST-LAID PLANS GO AWRY

THE SUMMER FOR TYLER Miller, an almost fifth grader, had been long, boring, and uneventful so far. Today was going to be a game-changer. Tyler and his dad were going on a weeklong white water rafting, hiking, and camping trip that would rival the summer vacations most of his friends at Woodland Park Elementary would have.

Shortly after Valentine's Day, Mr. and

Mrs. Miller decided to separate. The news was not a surprise to most, yet Tyler took it hard. He had managed to bypass the constant arguing and hold steadfast to the happy moments created as a family. His dad had been living in an apartment not far from his law office for the last six months, so Tyler was really looking forward to their time together. When his dad suggested the trip, Tyler went into immediate planning mode for what he would need to take. Tyler even found an old dusty duffle bag in the attic to carry his stuff.

Now the day of the trip had finally arrived. Tyler was kneeling on the couch, arms resting on the back cushion, staring intently out the window, waiting for his dad's arrival. This trip would be their first quality time together since the separation, and Tyler craved it. The relationship between him and his mom had become strained since the breakup. No matter how much she tried to make life as normal as possible, resentment had crept into their relationship. Tyler ultimately blamed his mom for his dad's departure, even though, deep inside, he knew it wasn't really her fault.

"Tyler, you're sure you've packed all the essentials?" Mrs. Miller asked, placing a tote full of snacks beside his duffle bag.

"Yeah—it's all in there," answered Tyler, looking down at his watch. His dad was twenty minutes behind schedule.

"Toothpaste, toothbrush, floss, blanket, canteen, hiking boots, socks, bathing suit, mosquito repellent, shorts, shirts, underwear . . . " Mom rattled off.

"Oops, I forgot something," interrupted Tyler, springing from the couch and making his way up the stairs to his room. He had no choice but to leave his post and retrieve the forgotten item.

Tyler had not yet reached his room when his mom called out, "Tyler, your dad just pulled into the driveway!"

"It figures!" Tyler dashed to the edge of the landing so his mom could hear him better. "Tell him I'll be right out, and, Mom, please don't mess it up!" Tyler yelled down the stairs before returning to his mission. Tyler's last few words began to gnaw at him. He regretted saying them, but he would have to deal with the amends when he returned from his trip.

Tyler beelined to his dresser. His mom's meddling proved beneficial today with her checklist reminder. A smirk appeared on his face, but it quickly changed to a frown. He opened the top drawer. It was empty. He opened drawer after drawer, just in case his underwear had found a new home, until he remembered his failure to put away the week's laundry, part of his summer chores. Shoving back the few items of clothing that had become disheveled during his frantic search, Tyler closed the last drawer and ran toward the laundry room. As he grabbed a handful of underwear, he accidentally knocked over a pile of neatly folded towels. Anticipating his mom's relentless complaints about not doing his chores, he put down the pile of underwear and began refolding the towels. They didn't look as good as his mom's folding efforts, but it was good enough for the moment. To ease the bit of guilt he was feeling about what he said to her, Tyler decided to go the extra mile and deliver the towels to the hall linen closet before starting down the stairs.

Halfway down the stairs Tyler realized that he had forgotten his underwear again! A quick trip for a forgotten item had turned into a tedious task. He took the stairs two at a time, grabbed the underwear, and shook off his frustration. He ran down the stairs and directly to his duffle bag. He unzipped it just wide enough to stuff in the pile of underwear. Grabbing the two bags, Tyler hustled his way to the front door. He opened the door in time to see his father's car race down the road. His mom was standing at the edge of the walkway, shaking her head.

"Wait! Where's Dad going? Did he forget something? I could have gone with him. How long will it take him before he comes back?" Tyler called out, trying to make sense of what had just happened.

"Honey," Mrs. Miller said, doing her best to remain calm.

"Mom, what just happened? Did you two get into another fight? I can't believe this! Where's my cell phone? I can fix this!" Tyler said, dropping his two bags and running inside to find his cell phone, which once belonged to his dad.

Mrs. Miller followed behind him, carrying his duffle bag and the tote. "Honey, stop! I need you to listen to me," she pleaded.

"No! I don't have any time to waste. Dad needs to answer his phone!"

"Tyler, please stop," her voice was calm yet serious. "I need you to listen to me."

"No, Mom! I need to speak with Dad. It's ringing," Tyler said, trying to figure out what he would say when his dad answered.

"Honey, stop. He's not—"

"Ugh, straight to voicemail! Mom, what happened? I was only gone for a few minutes! What did you say?"

Mrs. Miller placed her hands on her son's shoulders. Tyler was agitated, but after several moments of silence, his shoulders slumped, and his gaze shifted toward the floor. Mrs. Miller sighed. "I didn't say anything, honey. Your dad had a last-minute work emergency, so he had to cancel the trip for now. He said he would make it up to you. He's very sorry, and I am too."

Mrs. Miller did her best to maintain her fragile composure by suggesting a temporary fix. "Why don't we go see a movie or grab a sundae."

"But, Mom, this was supposed to be the best trip ever—just the guys. Those were his exact words, Mom. How could you let him do this to me?" Tyler's voice quivered from the disappointment he was trying to mask.

"I'm sorry, Ty. It's okay to be upset. Maybe your dad will be able to plan something over the Labor Day weekend." Mrs. Miller tried her best to comfort him, though she knew her efforts would fall short.

Tyler fell into his mom's arms, and tears

began to stream down his face. He had looked forward to this trip since the first mention of it, and Tyler had relentlessly bragged about it to all his friends. This trip was going to fix everything. Tyler had concocted a master plan that would help bring his parents back together. How could one emergency cancel six months of planning? This couldn't be happening. How would he explain the cancelation to his friends, especially since they doubted the trip from the start? Jackson, a former best friend, would have a field day with this news. The first day of fifth grade should be epic, but now the odds of that were no longer in his favor.

CHAPTER 1

Late August

FIRST DAY OF FIFTH GRADE

I HAD BEEN TRYING to distance myself from the negative thoughts that have preoccupied my mind since that dreaded day earlier this month when Dad canceled our trip. No matter how hard I tried, I couldn't shake the disappointment. Mom was up late working on one of those silly signs she has me hold every first day of school since Pre-K. I had hoped the separation would change this routine, but she was more determined than ever to make life as normal as possible. Here lies the problem. Life hasn't been normal since Dad left almost seven months ago.

I looked at the digital clock on my nightstand. The alarm was about to sound, but I had been awake for nearly an hour. I heard Mom in the kitchen starting the traditional first day of school breakfast. She barely had any rest—all this effort for nothing. I wasn't hungry, and I certainly wasn't looking forward to school. I canceled the alarm and made myself get out of bed. Ideas were scrolling through my mind as I got dressed. Could I pretend to be sick? Stomach bugs always surface during the first week of school. Last year Olivia Butler never made it on the bus. She barfed all over her new shoes just as the bus pulled up to our stop. Yep, she had the stomach bug. But even if I could get out of school today and maybe the next few days, I had no way out. Not really.

I could already hear Jackson's remarks. He's the kind of kid everyone likes, yet somehow he could make you feel worthless without saying much. I think it has to do with his body language and the looks he gives. It happened to me several times last year, and I never saw it coming when he did it. The last time it happened, we were working on a STEM project.

There were five of us in our group, including Jackson. During the brainstorming part of the engineering process, we had to take a turn sharing a possible solution. Jackson was the first to share his idea, which was pretty good. I shared last, which was fine because no one had thought of my solution yet. Seth, Nicole, and Lacey, the other group members, seemed to like my idea best, and for about fifteen seconds, there was a buzz of excitement within our group's circle. Jackson's words came quick and sharp when he said, "It won't work." Instantly, silence fell over the group, and the next thing I knew, we were planning how to execute Jackson's idea. I honestly couldn't tell you how the shift happened, but it did. Jackson got his way, and the rest of us were along for the ride.

During the next forty minutes, the team worked together, but everyone avoided making eye contact with me. I did my best to shake it off, but a sick feeling settled in my gut. While lying in bed that night, I replayed the events in my mind. I couldn't figure out how Jackson did it, but he managed to make me feel inadequate, and the feeling lasted for days.

There was always the slim chance that Jackson would not be in my class for fifth grade, but year after year, we always have been in the same class. I had been glad about that—at least until the middle of fourth grade. That's when things changed. Until then, we were inseparable, and, surprisingly, not one teacher fussed when we asked to sit beside each other. We knew how to stay on task, and we communicated in code to avoid getting into trouble. We created the secret code during the summer after second grade and added more to it each summer. This summer was the first time we hadn't worked on it.

The smell of French toast and scrambled eggs drifted into my bedroom as I was getting ready. Mom would call me to come down to breakfast any minute now. I filled my old backpack with the bag of school supplies Mom brought home from the Back-to-School Bash we attended a few weeks ago at church. This is the first year that Mom didn't buy me a new backpack and lunchbox. When Dad left, Mom said money would be tight for a while, but I didn't think it would last this long. I loved the Minecraft-themed backpack last year, but this year, well, not so much. Most of my friends were getting Under Armour backpacks for fifth grade, but Mom said she had no choice but to spend the budgeted money on new clothes since I had a growth spurt.

"Ty, breakfast is on the table!" Mom said as she passed my bedroom to grab her camera. I took a deep breath, grabbed my backpack, and headed to the kitchen. My anxiety about the day had dampened my hunger, but the closer I got to the kitchen, the better Mom's breakfast feast smelled.

I managed to eat two large pieces of French toast and a heaping scoop of scrambled eggs. Mom even put out the real maple syrup that Grandma Sato, my mother's mom, brought back from her trip to Vermont in April. She tagged along with Grandpa Sato, who was there on business. The syrup tasted great with the French toast and eggs.

"You may want to brush your teeth before I take your first day of fifth grade pictures," Mom said, beginning to clear the dishes off the table.

"Is there a chance we can skip the pictures this year?" I asked, hoping Mom would concede. The look on her face said it all. Photos will be happening. I hurried to brush my teeth, so I could get this ritual over and done.

By the time I got back, the table was clear, and Mom had an assortment of props in hand. She outdid herself this year. It was as if Pinterest had a party in our kitchen. She was excited, so I decided to give in and let her have the moment. The recent changes in our home hadn't been easy on her either. If only I hadn't bragged so much about the trip that never happened. But there's no going back.

"Tilt your head to the right and lower your chin a little. Good. Now smile!"

From all the new directives, it was evident that Mom had watched too many YouTube tutorials this summer. The busier she stayed, the less she thought about Dad's departure. And, boy, did she stay busy.

I looked down at my watch and realized that it was time to leave. "Mom, we need to hurry, or I'll be late for the first day," I said before realizing that being late would not be so bad, especially today. I could avoid talking to anyone at least until recess or lunch, whichever came first. Too late. Mom put down the camera, grabbed her car keys, and headed for the car. The caffeine from her countless cups of coffee had kicked in. I hesitated a second, then grabbed my recycled backpack and followed her. Ready or not, here it comes.

CHAPTER 2

First Day of Fifth Grade

JACKSON UNLEASHED

ALTHOUGH I WAS LOOKING forward to having Mrs. Parker as my fifth grade teacher, I was not thrilled to see Jackson enter the classroom along with several other familiar students. They were talking excitedly, most likely catching up on all the summer happenings. I continued unloading the school supplies from my backpack and avoided making eye contact with anyone, but it didn't take long before I heard my name from across the room.

"Hey, Tyler! We're in the same class

again," Jackson said. "How was the big camping trip?" He was talking as he searched for his name on the spotless desktops grouped in sets of six. I had failed to check if he was part of my table group. Once I spotted my name, I took my seat and didn't look any further. I pretended not to hear him and continued organizing my desk contents.

From the corner of my eye, I saw Jackson stop at a group of desks toward the front of the room. He started to drop his backpack on the chair. I felt some relief. Then Jackson laughed, grabbed his backpack, and said, "I guess we have a Jack and a Jackson in our class this year."

I quickly scanned the name tags on the desks in my group. My heart sank to my feet when I spotted Jackson's name. Not only was he in my class, his desk was two seats away from me. The knot in my stomach grew tighter, and the hairs on my neck stood on end as I felt his breath on my neck.

"Hey, Tyler! Didn't you hear me say your name when I entered the classroom?"

"Oh, sorry, I guess I was focusing on unloading my backpack."

"Going deaf already! Maybe you still have water in your ears from the white water rafting you did earlier this month. Hey, why are you using the same backpack as last year? I told you we were all buying Under Armour ones for fifth grade. Minecraft is so last year."

"Yeah, I know. My mom ran out of time." I said it even though it was a lie.

"Well, don't wait too long. You don't want everyone to think you're a dork or a loser. I can't wait to hear about the big trip. You couldn't stop bragging about it, so it's time to share the details. You can tell us all about it during recess."

"Sounds good," I said, hoping I could figure out how to get out of recess.

The classroom clatter settled down as Mrs. Parker made her way to the front of the room. She smiled and waited for the tardy bell to finish ringing before talking.

"Welcome to fifth grade! I'm Mrs. Parker, and we will spend the next few weeks reviewing class and school-wide expectations and getting to know one another. Summer break brings many opportunities for exciting experiences. This summer, my husband and I traveled to the Serengeti to witness the great migration. The Serengeti or Serengeti National Park is located in Tanzania, a country in eastern Africa. We saw herds of lions, buffalo, leopards, elephants, and rhinos, known as the "top five." My husband is a photojournalist and captured the most amazing photos that I hope to share with you soon."

Mrs. Parker's words mesmerized the class. I could tell by looking around that everyone couldn't wait to hear more.

"Enough from me for the moment," Mrs. Parker said. "It's time to hear from some of you. Who would like to share an exciting summer experience?"

"I'm sure Tyler is dying to share about his epic white water rafting camping trip. I'm Jackson, by the way, but most of my friends call me Jax," Jackson blurted out.

"Okay, thank you for the information, Jackson, or should I call you Jax?"

"Jax is fine, Mrs. Parker. And I'm sure the whole class is excited to hear about Tyler's trip," he said, giving her a cheesy smile.

"White water rafting sounds adventurous! Tyler, do you mind sharing?" Mrs. Parker asked, giving me a hopeful look.

"I . . . I . . . . guess I can," I said as I tried to remember some of the details from the website I researched earlier this summer.

"Please make your way to the front of the room, Tyler."

Mrs. Parker extended her arm in my direction, and I had no choice but to comply. My heart started pounding as I made my way to the front of the classroom. I bet the students in the first few rows could see the pulse in my neck. I stood quietly for ten seconds, taking several deep breaths. I decided to make it up as I went. Chances are no one will know any better, especially Jackson. Or Jax. Since when does anyone call him Jax? I straightened my shoulders and began.

"My dad and I spent a week white water rafting the Owlhee River and exploring the great surroundings. Once we set up our campsite, we went hiking down some cool paths and explored many great waterfalls. Traveling down the rapids, we spotted many wild animals like . . . umm, raptors, antelope, umm . . . beavers, sheep, ostrich—no, I mean otters, and coyotes." I was trying to recall the entire list from the internet.

"That sounds like an amazing trip, Tyler. Does anyone have any comments or questions for Tyler?" Mrs. Parker asked, scanning the room. "Yes, Jax."

"Don't you mean, Owyhee River?" Jackson asked, looking quite smug.

"Oh, yeah . . . I forgot how to say it."

A girl in the second row raised her hand, and I called on her.

"What do you mean by raptors?" Melanie asked.

"Uhm, raptors are . . . " I searched for an answer, but I'm not sure what the internet meant when it listed raptors. "They're like . . . uhm, kinda like modern-day dinosaurs."

"Dinosaurs! Are you sure you actually went on this epic trip? It sure doesn't sound like you know what you're talking about!" Jackson blurted out, causing Mrs. Parker to intervene.

"Now, Jax, it's not easy talking in front of a group. Sometimes nerves get the best of us. Tyler is doing his best, especially being the first volunteer."

I watched Jackson's reaction. I had seen this look before. He was not buying my story. He won't let this go, especially after I made such a big deal about this trip. Why did I have to brag so much about it?

Mrs. Parker walked over to me, placed her hand on my shoulder, and thanked me for sharing. All the great things I heard about her seem to be true.

"Let's have another volunteer . . . Jax, why don't you go next," Mrs. Parker said, giving me a wink.

"Sure!" Jax said and quickly made his way to the front of the room. "Since Tyler spent so much time bragging about his epic summer trip before school ended in fourth grade, my family and I decided to take the same trip to the Owyhee River during the last week of July. We camped in Anderson Crossing and spent our days fishing for trout, exploring trails and waterfalls, horseback riding, and observing wildlife. The raptors Tyler referred to are amazing birds of prey like turkey vultures, bald eagles, osprey, and various hawks, including the rough-legged hawk, and my favorite—the red-tailed hawk. By night, we explored the starry skies from our campground. We used the Night Sky app on our phones to identify the stars and constellations. They were the brightest stars I've ever seen. My dad said the stars appeared brighter because we were so far away from all the city lights. The whole trip was amazing, and I will never forget any of the details. I guess you really have to experience something to remember it," Jax said, turning his smirk in my direction.

"Thank you, Jax. Does anyone have any comments or questions for Jax?"

Mrs. Parker pointed to a boy in the back row.

"My name is Jamal, and I'm new to Woodland Creek. Jax, your summer vacation sounds incredible. Why is the red-tailed hawk your favorite?"

"It's my favorite because it looks like it's not even trying to fly. It floats through the air without having to do much work," Jax responded.

"Cool!" Jamal exclaimed.

The sharing continued for the next thirty minutes, but I stopped listening after Jackson's surprise reveal. My thoughts flooded with all the possible things I'm sure Jackson will say to me during recess. There's no doubt in my mind that he knows I didn't go on the trip, and I'll probably hear about it for weeks. After a short stretch break, Mrs. Parker began reviewing our daily schedule. Whew, recess is after lunch. I have three hours before I need to worry about Jackson, so I decided to give my attention back to Mrs. Parker. At least she is nice.

CHAPTER 3

TAKE THE ENEMY BY SURPRISE

I SAT NEXT TO a few new students during lunch, avoiding Jackson as much as possible. Jackson sat at the far end of the long table. It appeared that he had made some new friends. Jamal, Melanie, Eric, Henry, and Amy surrounded him as he continued sharing the details of his summer trip. It's not fair. I should be the one sharing about this trip. Why did he have to copy me? And why did Dad mess it all up?

I watched the group's reactions as Jackson continued talking, and I felt angry. I was so mad at Dad. He was so selfish. Now I'm the one who has to face the embarrassment.

Adults don't care. Dad doesn't care. Why do grown-ups think kids will just get over disappointments? That was probably true when I was three, maybe four, but not as a fifth grader. If Dad really loved me, he should have canceled his emergency and not our trip!

Lunch was over too soon, and it was time for us to clean up our areas and head to recess. I managed to avoid Jackson or Jax all morning, but I knew he was coming for me at recess. As I zipped my lunchbox, I heard him say to Jamal, "I think we should ask Tyler more about his trip to Owyhee River; that's if he really went." The others laughed as they walked past me to line up. I was dreading the next thirty minutes.

Jackson and several others gathered around me before I could join in on some of the recess games, and the questions started.

"So, Tyler, did you really go on your epic trip? Because it sounds like you were sharing details from the internet."

"Yeah, of course, I went!" My voice cracked as I tried to mask the uneasy feeling growing inside me.

"Oh yeah? Then describe the camp area," Jackson said, moving closer to me.

Why can't he drop the whole thing? I felt

anger growing inside me from the embarrassment Jackson was stirring up. For a moment I wished I could close my eyes and make myself disappear. It was a silly thought, but it's all I've got. Wait, what if I try to think of something embarrassing to say about Jackson?

Suddenly, I remembered a secret about him, so I took a deep breath and began speaking. "The drive was fun. Dad and I chatted about his own experience in fifth grade. Back then, elementary schools went up to sixth grade, so my dad didn't feel the same way since he had two more years to go before junior high. Yep, that's what they used to call middle school back then. We stopped at a tourist spot before heading to the campground. It was an old-fashioned diner that my dad used to visit when he went camping with his family. It was so cool inside. Instead of eating dinner, we ordered waffle sundaes. They were so good! Later, when we arrived at the campground, Dad set up our large tent beside the river, and I rolled out my new sleeping bag, even though my other one wasn't that old. We had to buy a new one before our trip because the old one stunk from when Jackson peed himself during a sleepover at my house! I should have known better. Jackson usually wets his bed at least once a week! Oops, sorry, Jackson, I mean Jax. I didn't mean to tell everyone your secret!"

My voice carried beyond the group, and several students began laughing and pointing toward Jackson. The conversation moved to Jackson's unfortunate problem. Suddenly, I was not the center of attention, and Jax was . . . crying. Really? Maybe he'll mind his own business the next time. And just like that, no one was worried if I really went on the white water rafting trip. The embarrassment stopped, and I no longer felt the need to disappear.

CHAPTER 4

Early September

I DON'T WANT TO TALK ABOUT IT

TODAY IS THE DAY after Labor Day, and we're back in school after a lousy three-day weekend. Not only did Dad not care enough to reschedule our camping trip, he didn't even try to show up for the annual block party. The neighbors asked about him, and Mom made up some lame excuses. Why did she even bother? Mom still believed Dad was going to come home, and we would be a happy family again. She said the same thing every week. "Dad needs a little time to adjust to his new job. Being a successful lawyer is very stressful. His boss is very demanding, so we need to be patient. He'll be back. You'll see." I wanted to believe it would happen, but Dad's actions weren't showing that.

The morning just dragged on. My focus was not on school. I kept thinking about how Dad let me down when I needed him most. Fifth grade should be the best year in elementary. So far, it had been far from that.

I decided to concentrate more on learning to keep my mind off things I cannot change, no matter how hard I tried. After a brief introduction, Mrs. Parker showed us a clip about Ellis Island, located in New York Harbor, during the early 1900s. That caught my attention. She said that twelve million immigrants came to America through Ellis Island from 1892 to 1924. That's about 375,000 immigrants a year, if my math was correct. It sounded exciting and scary at the same time. The video said that many immigrants were separated from their families and sent back to their homeland.

On the morning of November 12, 1954, the doors of Ellis Island opened for the last time as an immigration station. Ellis Island is a museum now, located not too far from the

Statue of Liberty. I think I will put it on my list of places to visit before I finish college, especially since I just remembered Grandpa Sato mentioning that his father came from Japan through Ellis Island a few years before World War II. It didn't mean much to me at the time, because I didn't know anything about Ellis Island, but now I'm interested in finding out more. I'll ask Mom if I can call Grandpa Sato tonight to get more information and maybe convince him to plan a visit to the Ellis Island Museum. That would be a great family trip to take. Mrs. Parker will think it's cool that I have a connection to Ellis Island. I think I will tell her during lunch.

"I would like you to form groups of four to begin researching more about Ellis Island," Mrs. Parker said as she rolled the iPad cart to the center of the room. "Each group will be given a set of questions to answer and a few iPads. The answers are found on the Ellis Island site I will post on the whiteboard. Once you pick your group, please come up and grab your materials. I'll be available to help if you have questions."

Students began moving about the room, and groups formed quickly. Jackson hasn't talked to me since the playground incident, so I don't expect to be part of his group, which is a good thing. It looks like I have to join a group of three from across the room. Mrs. Parker motioned me to come over. I hesitated for a second when I spotted Jenna. She's a talker and always asks so many questions—time to get this activity over and done.

"Hey, Ty! It's been a while since we've been in a group together," Jenna said as I joined the group.

"Yeah, I guess," I said, grabbing the assignment sheet from the table and pretending to focus on reading the questions.

"Let's use the back table since no one is there," said Jenna. She started walking toward the table before anyone could comment. We followed her.

"Did you know my Irish ancestors came through Ellis Island in the late 1800s? My Grandma O'Toole says I get my beautiful fiery red hair from my great-great-grandmother Fiona. Do any of you have ancestors that arrived through Ellis Island?" Jenna asked.

"No, I don't think I do," Megan said.

"Maybe," said James, "I'm not really sure."

"What about you, Tyler?" Jenna asked.

"Actually, you're not the only one with ancestors who came through Ellis Island. My great, great, no, maybe one great . . . anyway, my mom's grandfather Sato came from Japan through Ellis Island," I said. "That makes him my great-grandfather."

"Cool," said James.

"And what about your dad's family?" Jenna asked.

"What about them?"

"Where are they from?"

"I'm not sure."

"Can you ask him?" she asked.

"Who?"

"Your dad, silly!"

"No! I mean, he's too busy," I said, hoping she would drop all the questions.

"I'm sure he's not always busy. Ask him during dinner. Don't you want to know where your dad's family came from? Aren't you a little curious?"

"No, not really! Can we drop it and get started on the assignment?"

"Why not?"

"Why not? Why don't you mind your own business and stop asking me all these questions!" I said, aggravated by her persistence.

"I just thought . . . "

"You talk too much. Always have and probably always will! Did you inherit that from your great-great-grandmother O'Toole?"

Jenna's eyes instantly filled with tears, and her face turned every shade of red. She wiped her eyes with her shirt sleeve and excused herself to use the restroom. When she returned, we completed the assignment without another sound from her. It's the quietest she's been in years. Mission accomplished!

CHAPTER 5

LATER THAT EVENING

WHILE MOM WAS COOKING dinner, I began working on my homework. I didn't expect it would take too long to finish. Mrs. Parker was not one of those teachers who believed in giving tons of homework. Ironically, since Dad moved out, there's not much to do in the afternoons, so I wouldn't mind extra work to keep my mind off my lousy situation.

Mom worked two jobs these days and was always catching up on laundry or paying bills after she got home. Dinner time used to be a feast. Mom made lasagna, homemade pizza, teriyaki chicken with rice, or some other delicious recipe that she thought might be fun to try. Lately, we've been mainly eating frozen chicken strips or fish sticks that I dip into Ranch dressing. Nothing we eat is home-made—just something out of a bag from the freezer. I didn't mind at first, but I do now. Dad has messed up all the great things about our family, and the more I think about it, the angrier it makes me.

Part of me felt terrible for what I said to Jenna today, but part of me didn't. She brought it on herself when she didn't listen to me. I told her to drop it, but she didn't. She kept talking and talking. After Dad let me down again this weekend, I didn't want to talk about him, especially to her or anyone else in that group.

Why couldn't she see that? It's not anyone's business what goes on in my home. The last thing I needed was everyone talking about me behind my back because they felt sorry for me. The more I thought about it, the less bad I felt about what I said. I don't like feeling uncomfortable or embarrassed in front of others, so people need to learn to stay in their lane, as my uncle Danny often said.

I can smell the chicken strips, which meant dinner was almost ready. I also smelled whiffs of mac 'n' cheese. It wasn't lasagna, but hey, it was something different.

"Ty, dinner is ready," Mom said as she stuck her head into my bedroom.

"Can I eat dinner in my room tonight?" I hoped she would let me.

"I thought we could eat together on the patio. We didn't use it much this summer," she said.

"I still have some homework to do."

"I thought Mrs. Parker didn't believe in giving much homework."

"She doesn't. I . . . I guess I'm tired, and that's why it's taking me longer to get it finished." I hoped this answer would satisfy her curiosity.

"That's normal. It always takes a few weeks to get used to being back at school. I was hoping for some company, but maybe tomorrow. I'll bring you a plate in a few minutes."

"Thanks, Mom! And don't forget—"

"The Ranch dressing! Yep, I'm on it."

"Thanks, Mom! You're the best!"

I was glad Mom was okay with me eating in my room tonight. I wasn't in the mood to have any conversations, especially if they were about Dad.

CHAPTER 6

October 31st, early morning

NO PLANS EQUALS NO FUN

IT WAS HALLOWEEN, AND I had completely dropped the ball on getting a costume. Mom asked me a few weeks ago if I had any costume ideas, but nothing had come to mind. Now I wished I had planned better. I heard noises coming from the kitchen, so I went to investigate. Mom was sitting at the counter, and her sewing machine was humming as she was busy sewing something.

"Hey, Ty! I'm almost finished with your costume," Mom said.

"My costume?"

"Yes, I've been working on it for the last few days."

"But I never told you what I wanted to be."

"No, you didn't, so I decided for you."

"What? Mom, I hope you didn't make something babyish."

"Are you saying you're too old for Peter Pan or Buzz Lightyear?"

"Mom, are you kidding . . ."

"Calm down, Ty! Yes, I'm only kidding. I found some of your dad's old army fatigues and decided to alter them to fit you. You're going to be a combat soldier!"

"Really? That's pretty cool, Mom! But wait, won't Dad be upset if he finds out that you used some of his fatigues?"

"Relax. I talked to your dad about it earlier this week. He's happy to let you use his fatigues. Anyway, I don't think they'll fit your dad anymore. He was much trimmer when he was younger. What do you think?" Mom asked, holding up the finished costume.

"Those are so cool! Thanks, Mom!"

"You might as well try them on before you get dressed for school."

"Good idea."

I grabbed the fatigues from Mom and ran back to my room to try them on. As I buttoned the jacket, I wondered how Dad felt when he wore this uniform in the Army. I ran to my closet and grabbed my boots and pulled them on.

"Hey, Mom! They fit perfectly!"

"Hold on. I'm coming," Mom said.

She arrived with a patrol cap in hand and proceeded to place it on my head. Before I could turn to look in the mirror, I saw that Mom was crying. Not an ugly cry, just a few tears streaming down her face.

"Mom, what's wrong?"

"Nothing, honey. You look so much like your dad right now. Seeing you like this brings back many memories. Wow, your dad will do a double-take when he sees you in his fatigues."

"Are you going to send him a picture?"

"No need to. Your dad is planning to stop by this evening and take you Trick or Treating, as long as you don't think that's too babyish for you now that you are a fifth grader."

"Dad's coming? Really?"

"Yes, he's been planning on it all week."

"Thanks, Mom!" I plunged in to give her a big hug.

"Of course, honey. Your dad is always welcome here."

"I know, but I thought . . ." I didn't know how to express my feelings, so I didn't say anything else. I just kept hugging Mom.

"It's all good, kiddo, but we better put it in high gear before you're late for school!"

"What's Dad planning to wear?"

"He's picking up some new fatigues from the Army and Navy Surplus store not far from his office. You will be twins!"

"Really? That's so cool, Mom! I can't wait to tell my friends!"

"Clock's ticking, Tyler! Change into your school clothes while I get breakfast ready. You'll have to eat it in the car, so I'll keep it simple today."

"No problem, Mom. I'm almost too excited to eat!"

As I hurried to get dressed, I couldn't stop thinking about how cool Dad and I will look tonight. It's been almost three months since Dad canceled the big summer trip, so I can't wait to spend time with him. Suddenly, my thoughts flooded with all sorts of questions. Will it be weird to hang out with Dad after all this time? Will we have anything to talk about?

Has Dad changed? Does he still love Mom? Does he still love me? Will he come back home so we can be a family again?

I grabbed my backpack and headed to the garage where Mom was waiting. No time to worry about all the questions now. It's going to be a great Halloween. Even though I didn't plan ahead, I'm sure glad Mom did.

CHAPTER 7

October 31st

ALL IS GOOD UNTIL IT'S NOT

SCHOOL STARTED OUT WELL today. The best day in fifth grade so far. I felt hopeful for the first time. Mrs. Parker was dressed up as her favorite book character, Mary Poppins. I didn't know until today that Mary Poppins was a real book character from a series of books first published in the 1930s. Mrs. Parker looked identical to the movie character. She even had an umbrella with a parrot head on the handle. The whole class couldn't stop staring at her, and we kept noticing more details about her costume as the morning moved along.

During recess, I decided to tell Jackson about my Halloween costume. Sometimes friends have a falling out, but good friends always make up. We were good friends for years, so I owed it to him and to me too. I should never have told everyone about his problem. It was not a cool thing to do, no matter how upset he made me. I wanted to apologize so many times, but then I would convince myself that he had it coming. Today, knowing that Dad and I were finally going to spend time together, I felt it was the right time to fix things between us.

"Hey, Jackson. Can we talk?" I walked toward the court where Jackson was shooting baskets.

"I don't think we have anything to talk about," he said, avoiding any eye contact.

"Okay, I get that you're upset with me."

"Upset? I don't think that's the right word. You shared personal information. Good friends don't do that to each other!"

"And you don't think you did anything wrong?"

"What? Just because I called you out on a lie didn't give you the right to tell everyone about my problem. By the way, I no longer have that problem. Not that it's any of your business."

"That's good. I mean, it's good that your problem is no longer a problem. I didn't lie—"

"Come on, Ty, you lied about the whole trip!"

"That's because, well, it's hard to explain. I didn't want to, but it was . . . "

"It was what? Just say it!"

"It was . . . well, your fault."

"Huh? Are you serious? How is lying about your big white water rafting trip that you bragged about for weeks my fault?" he asked, glaring at me.

"Forget it; you'll never understand," I said, trying to avoid an uncomfortable conversation.

"No, I want to know. Tell me, or we're done as friends."

"You're right. We're done as friends. I'm sorry I wasted my time trying to fix things."

"Whatever! After what you did, I don't think I could ever be your friend again."

"Good! You've been a lousy friend since the middle of fourth grade. I don't even know why I stayed friends with the pee-pee boy for so long."

"I told you that it's not a problem any-more!"

"Yeah, but how do I know you're not lying?" I asked, sniffing the air. "I can still smell your pee."

Jackson stopped bouncing the basketball and turned his back to me. I could tell he was upset, but I decided not to say or do anything. I didn't smell anything except the pile of leaves scattered around the playground, but I'd never admit it. Once again, he brought this on himself. I wanted to fix things between us and tell him about my Halloween costume, but he ruined it. My thoughts shifted to Trick or Treating and Dad. Five minutes after Dad arrives, Jackson will no longer matter.

CHAPTER 8

October 31st — early evening

TRICK OR TREATING FIXES EVERYTHING

MRS. PARKER GAVE US a homework-free night, so I didn't have to spend any time completing math or reading. Instead, I began searching the internet on how to apply camouflage face paint. Dad and I needed to look authentic. He probably still remembered how to apply the face camouflage, but I didn't want to waste a minute of our time together. Mom bought some camo face paint at Walmart that matched the fatigues. I asked her not to call it makeup, but she laughed and said that war paint was a type of makeup. I guess she's right, but it sounded wrong.

I found some cool tutorials and began practicing on my face. After a few attempts, I think I got the perfect face camouflage. I will be one with the fatigues. I was glad I had taken off my polo shirt before applying the war paint. It took me less than five minutes to get fully dressed—fatigues, boots, and cap. I ran to the mirror to make a final inspection. Authentic, that's the word that comes to mind.

"Hey, Mom, come and see," I shouted.

"I'm coming."

After a minute, Mom walked into my room carrying a photo. It was a picture of Dad wearing fatigues. Mom said he was about nineteen when the photo was taken. I can't believe how much we look alike, other than the Japanese features that I inherited from my mom's side of the family. Dad's going to flip when he sees his twin.

"Tyler, you did a great job with the makeup."

"Mom! It's war paint, not makeup."

"Sorry, you did a great job with the war paint."

"That's better! Hey, what time is Dad getting here?"

"He should be here soon. He mentioned something about a surprise in his text."

"What do you think the surprise will be?"

"Honestly, I really don't know. Maybe your dad found the time to find his dog tags and duffle bag from Grandma and Grandpa Miller's house. They've been packed in a trunk in their attic for years."

"Wow, I hope that's the surprise. Those will be the final touches to our great outfits, and think about all the candy we can stuff into a duffle bag. We'll be eating candy for months!"

"I'm sure your dentist will not be happy about that!"

"Aww, Mom, it's Halloween. The last person I want to think about on Halloween is my dentist. You sure know how to ruin the moment," I said, trying not to break a smile. The truth is nothing can ruin this moment. Not Jackson, a dentist, or anyone else. When Dad gets here, it's going to make everything better.

I heard the faint ring of the doorbell. Dad was here. I didn't waste any time. I handed Mom Dad's picture and ran toward the stairs. The doorbell rang again.

I shouted, "I'm coming, Dad!"

I imagined how Dad would look in the

new fatigues, carrying the duffle bag, and wearing the dog tags around his neck. I got to the door and took a deep breath before opening it. Wait, are these Trick or Treaters? For a second, I didn't realize it was my dad. He was dressed like a pirate, and he was holding a little boy wearing a similar pirate costume. I've never seen this little boy before, and my thoughts began spinning in all directions.

"Hey, big guy!" he said.

"Hey, Dad." I was still trying to understand why my dad was wearing a pirate costume. I don't think he even noticed that I was wearing his old fatigues.

"This little guy here is Drew, the fiercest and most adventurous pirate on the Seven Seas! His crew jumped ship on him, so I invited him to join us tonight. I knew you wouldn't mind. After all, a pirate in need is a pirate indeed. On second thought, I'm not sure if that proverb works here, but you get the idea, big guy!"

"Uhm . . . hello, Drew. Cool costume," I managed to say, even though I felt my body growing numb.

"Arrr! It's Captain Drew! Do you need to walk the plank?" Drew asked as Dad set him down.

"Uhm, no, I'm good, Captain Drew," I answered, reluctantly. Who is this kid, and is this how it's going to be all night?

"What are you supposed to be? You sort of look like a swamp monster," Drew said.

"No, I'm not a swamp monster."

"He's an Army combat solider, Captain Drew!" Dad said.

"Oh. So if you're an Army guy, why do you have makeup all over your face?" Drew asked.

"No, it's not makeup . . . well, it is sort of, but it's face camouflage for soldiers," I said, hoping Mom would come to my rescue.

"Hi! Who do we have here?" Mom asked, appearing a bit puzzled.

"This is Captain Drew. He's joining Ty and me on our Trick or Treating adventures this evening."

"Hello, Captain Drew! I'm Private Tyler's mom, Mrs. Miller. You may call me Miss Jessica. Those are some impressive costumes both of you are wearing," Mom said, raising her eyebrow as if trying to look impressed.

I could tell Mom wasn't happy even though there was a smile plastered on her face. I've seen that smile before. It was almost real, but there was a hint of phony. If you looked closely, you could see the tension in the corners of her mouth.

"Yeah, Captain Drew's mom found them for us," said Dad.

"She must have some great connections. Hey, Tyler, why don't you show Captain Drew your room while I talk to your dad," Mom said.

"Oh, okay. Sure, let's go, Captain Drew."

"Arrr, there, matey!" Drew said, taking my hand. I didn't want to leave the room with Captain Drew. I wanted to hear what Mom was going to say to Dad. He hadn't even noticed how much I looked like him in his fatigues. He didn't say one word about it. I didn't see any sign of the army duffle bag or the dog tags that Mom mentioned earlier. Why did Dad bring this kid as a tagalong? Who is he? And why did Dad dress up like him and not like me? Why didn't he keep his promise? Is Dad dating Drew's mom? All these unanswered questions consumed my attention, and I no longer had any interest in Trick or Treating. A dull ache settled in my stomach.

As I showed Drew my room, I strained to listen to what Mom and Dad were saying downstairs. No matter how hard I tried to catch part of the conversation, Drew's squeals and pirate antics muffled any chance of making out even a random word. For a little kid, he was a real nuisance. Within minutes, all my Legos and model cars were sprawled across my bed and floor.

"Please don't touch that, Drew!"

"I told you, it's Captain Drew, and I can do anything I want or I'll make you walk the plank!"

"Whatever! You're a spoiled brat, Captain Drew!" I said before thinking about the harshness of my words.

"Ryan! Ryan! The swamp monster called me a brat!" Drew shouted as he ran out of my room. I followed behind him.

Drew slowed down as he tackled the stairs, giving me a few seconds to catch a part of my parents' conversation.

"I'm only helping a friend, that's all!" I heard Dad say.

"You should have warned me. I told Tyler that you were going to wear fatigues," Mom said, but she stopped talking when Drew ran to Dad and grabbed his leg.

"Ryan, he called me a brat!" Drew said, pointing in my direction.

"Ty, why would you do that?" Dad asked.

"Why? He made a mess of my room, that's why! Why does he even need to be here?" I asked, looking at Mom for answers.

"Your dad is helping a friend from work, honey. Drew's mom had an unexpected change of plans and has to work late tonight. Your dad thought you wouldn't mind if Drew tagged along. I'm sure you will all have a great time. Go grab a tote bag from the closet. I believe there's a camouflage one somewhere in the pile."

I can't believe what I am hearing. How is Mom okay with this? I can't believe Dad broke another promise. The dull ache in my stomach got worse.

"Mom, I think I'm going to be sick!" I made a mad dash to the hall bathroom.

A few seconds later, I heard a knock on the door.

"Ty, are you okay?" Mom asked.

"No, I think I have a stomach bug," I answered through the door.

"Oh no, honey! Maybe some Pepto Bismol will help. I'll go grab it for you."

Pepto Bismol will not help tonight. I know it, and I think Mom knows it too, but I didn't say a word. While Mom was getting the Pepto Bismol, I could hear Drew and Dad's conversation from behind the door.

"Let's go, Ryan! I want to go Trick or Treating now," Drew said.

"Just a minute, buddy. We need to wait for Tyler."

"No, I don't like him. He called me a brat, and he needs to walk the plank!"

"I'm sure he didn't mean it."

"Yes, he did! He needs to walk the plank! Let's go now!"

The conversation continued for a few more seconds but gradually became more distant. I looked at myself in the mirror and began to wash the war paint off my face. It was harder to get off than I expected, so I grabbed some toilet tissue and started rubbing. When I couldn't get any more off, I decided to come out of the bathroom. Dad and Drew were outside on the sidewalk talking to a group of Trick or Treaters. That explained the sudden silence. Mom appeared with the Pepto Bismol in hand. She looked at me but didn't say a word. She just hugged me.

"I'll tell your dad," she said.

"Thanks, Mom."

"By the way, I've got something to help

get the rest of the war paint off. Give me a few, and I'll bring it to your room."

I suddenly hated the fatigues I was wearing and couldn't wait to change out of them. I rushed to my room without saying goodbye to Dad and the little brat. Halloween was officially over!

CHAPTER 9

THE DAY AFTER HALLOWEEN SHOULD BE CANCELED

MY EYES POPPED OPEN a few minutes before the alarm was due to go off. Nothing in me wanted to start this day. I know I will be bombarded with questions I don't want to answer. Dad and I were finally going to spend some quality time together, and I was sure it would be epic. But once again, Dad was a big letdown. I wanted to hate him, but it's easier said than done. For most of my life, Dad has been there for me. I wish he hadn't taken that new job. It changed him, and not for the better. Sure, I guess he makes great money, but it doesn't make up for the disappointments we've faced because of Dad's schedule and the added stress.

Today is going to be brutal. Everyone will compare their candy stash to see who collected the biggest haul. Most kids exaggerate, but Dad and I for sure would have collected the most if all had gone as planned. Our costumes would have stood out, and people would have given us more candy because Dad is an actual military veteran. But no, Captain Drew ruined it. At least, that's what I am telling myself this morning. Yep, I hope that little brat gets a stomach ache every time he eats a piece of Halloween candy.

****

I didn't feel like eating breakfast this morning, but Mom still made me take a protein bar with me. She didn't say much on the way to school, and I was okay with the silence. As I walked toward my classroom, I didn't see Mrs. Parker standing outside the door as usual. When I walked into my classroom, a man greeted me instead of Mrs. Parker. A substitute. Not what I needed today.

"Hey, I'm Mr. Stevenson, your substitute. And you are?"

"Disappointed. No, sorry! I'm Tyler. Uhm, I meant to say I am disappointed that Mrs. Parker isn't here today." Whew, that was close. I didn't mean to say disappointed out loud. It just came out. That's been happening quite a bit lately.

"No worries, Tyler. I get it."

"Thanks, Mr. . . . Sorry, I didn't catch your name."

"Stevenson."

"That's right." I need to pull myself together.

"I guess all the sugar is fogging the brain!"

"Sugar?"

"Yeah, from all the Halloween candy. You do remember it was Halloween yesterday, right?"

I was speechless for several seconds as Mr. Stevenson waited on my answer. The Halloween interrogation had started, and I had no idea how I would get through this day. An idea popped into my head, and I decided to go with it.

"I'm not into Halloween anymore. It's for little kids."

"It's disappointing that you feel this way. I was hoping to share about my spectacular costume," Mr. Stevenson said.

"You went Trick or Treating?"

"Yes, the three of us. My wife, my daughter, and me. We were the talk of our neighborhood."

"Well, then I guess it's too bad that I think the whole thing is babyish." I was curious, but I wasn't about to give in. I did not need anything else to sabotage my day.

"Yes, too bad, but hey, it's all good. I guess part of me hasn't fully grown up yet," he said, adding a wink and playful smile.

Once again, I found myself unsure of what to do or say. It was a good thing that more students were filtering into the classroom, and Mr. Stevenson's attention diverted to them. I took the opportunity to get to my desk before anyone else asked questions. On the way, I grabbed a random book from the classroom library.

My plan was to bury my head in this book and not look up until I had no choice. I turned the book over to judge my pick. Not bad. *Diary of a Wimpy Kid.* I began reading and tried my best to tune out the voices surrounding me.

"Hey, Tyler," said Megan as she settled in at her desk. I pretended not to hear her and just kept reading. Megan reached over and tapped me on my arm, "Tyler, are you ignoring me?" I looked up pretending to be surprised by her remark.

"Huh?"

"I said, are you ignoring me?"

"No, I just didn't hear you. I'm really into this book."

Without hesitation, Megan snatched the book from my hands and after a quick glance at the page said, "You're only on page one. You're either an extremely slow reader or a big liar."

"What's your problem?" I could feel my anger rising.

"My problem? I don't have a problem. I was trying to be kind, something that you haven't been this school year," she said, slamming her binder on her desk.

"From where I'm sitting, it appears that you have more issues than me. Most of the time it's better if people mind their own business, especially if others are reading."

"You know, I give up! Forget I even said a word!"

"That's fine with me! Now can I have my book back?"

"Here, take your lousy book!" She tossed the book my way, and I caught it before it hit the floor. "Ugh! I don't even know who you are anymore."

"Good! It's better that way. Now if you and everyone else can leave me alone, maybe we can enjoy the rest of fifth grade."

"Is something wrong?" Mr. Stevenson asked as he approached our table.

"Nope," I responded without looking up.

"I'm not sure," Megan said. She looked flustered, and her eyes were glassy as if she was about to cry.

"How can I help, Tyler? Megan?" asked Mr. Stevenson.

"There's nothing to help, Mr. Stevenson. I'm fine and Megan, well, is just Megan."

"Huh? What is that supposed to mean?" she asked, her face now blotchy and red.

"You know."

"No, I don't know," she retorted.

"Do you care to explain?" Mr. Stevenson asked.

"No, not particularly," I said, while opening the book and scanning to find where I left off.

"You're mean, Tyler Miller," Megan said.

My patience was gone, and I could not stop the words that came out of my mouth.

"And you're a spoiled brat whose breath can empty a room."

"Tyler, that's highly inappropriate!" Mr. Stevenson said, taking the book from my hands.

"Yeah, I can't help if the truth hurts. Maybe it will help Megan feel better if you share your lame Halloween costume story with her!"

"That's enough, young man! I think your rudeness has earned you a trip to the office."

Good. Now I won't have to spend the day listening to Halloween stories and being asked questions I don't want to answer.

"Fine." I got up and started walking toward the classroom door.

"Hold on, I'm going to send you with a buddy," Mr. Stevenson said.

"Not necessary. I know the way, and the last time I checked, I'm no longer in kindergarten." I kept walking and tuned out the rest of the conversation.

On the way to the office, I saw Jackson and a few others coming down the hall. They were talking about their Halloween adventures and laughing as our eyes met. Is it a coincidence or are they laughing at me? Do they know what happened to me last night? Did Jackson see my dad with that little brat? He probably did, and now he's making fun of me. It's time to shut him down and turn the laughter at his expense. As we get closer I lean in and say, "Jax, I hope you didn't pee in your Halloween costume like you did in my sleeping bag! Or maybe you finally wore a pull-up diaper. Or better yet, did you dress like Captain Underpants? If not, you may want to consider that choice for next Halloween!"

Several students in the hall started laughing at my remarks as Jackson's face turned bright red. I kept walking toward the office. The first time I mentioned Jackson's unfortunate problem, I felt bad afterward and even tried to apologize. This time, well, it's hard to explain. Simply put, I was feeling a sense of satisfaction. No one is going to laugh at me or make me feel uncomfortable again. And that's a promise.

Mid-January

A VISIT TO THE PRINCIPAL'S OFFICE

THE VISITS TO PRINCIPAL Dalton's office had become a mainstay in my weekly routine in this not-so-awesome fifth grade year. I took my usual seat in the waiting area and stared out the window, avoiding the scowls from the receptionist who, a few weeks before Christmas, lectured me for twenty minutes on how bouts of meanness didn't reflect well on a young man with so much potential. I had to applaud her effort. At least she seemed to care. But like everyone else in my world, her efforts had grown less hopeful over time.

The low gray clouds that darkened the wintery sky boasted snow. It's definitely cold enough for a good snow. No school tomorrow! The schools in this area close at the mention of snow, even if it's just a dusting. I'm genuinely surprised that the big guys that sit in the district office not too far from my school haven't decided to dismiss early. A buzzer rang from the receptionist's desk. She peered out the window and then pressed the intercom button.

"Welcome to Woodland Park Elementary. How may I help you?" The scowl had disappeared, and her voice sounded pleasant.

"Hello, it's Mr. Pendleton. I'm here to sign out my children, Jarrod and Charlotte Pendleton. It's supposed to snow, and the bus will never make it down our street."

"No problem, Mr. Pendleton. Please come inside where it's warm, and I'll call for your children." She buzzed him in and at the same time, motioned me to head back to the principal's office. Mr. Dalton was waiting for me just outside his office door.

"You made it to Thursday this week, Tyler. Some might call that an improvement."

Mr. Dalton used sarcasm when he was

disappointed. I used to think he was the best principal, but not so much anymore. I'm pretty sure my name has been erased from his list of promising students. It had been there since I started at Woodland Park, but I guess things and people change. These days we tolerate one another. We stick to the facts, nothing more, nothing less. He typically stared down at his laptop and typed while I talked, and then I waited for the consequence. In the early days, Mr. Dalton would bring in the guidance counselor or call my mom for a conference. But when my visits became more frequent, he started just skimming through the behavior handbook, which was online these days and not an actual book, and picked out a consequence. I've done all the consequences—in-school suspension, out-of-school suspension, detention, work detail, notes of apology, Saturday school, and the list goes on. Today he walked over to his desk and flipped open his laptop. No surprise there.

"What happened today?" he asked, not looking up from his screen.

"I told Henry he was annoying."

"Is that it?" Mr. Dalton's face was still buried behind his computer.

"And he better stop stuffing his face before

his body gets too big for his desk."

In my opinion, I did Henry a favor. When we were in third grade, he was smaller than me, but his weight has more than doubled since his family opened the donut shop.

"Hmm." Mr. Dalton paused while he typed on his computer. When he finished, he hit print.

At this point, I could tell he was preparing a behavior referral parent letter.

Mr. Dalton grabbed the copies and handed one to me.

"Take this home for your mother to sign and come back to my office for lunch detention."

"Do you think we'll still be in school by lunchtime?" I asked, surprised by his choice of consequence.

"I haven't gotten a call from the district office yet, so like I said, I'll see you during lunch."

His phone rang just as I stood up to leave his office.

"Hello, Mr. Dalton speaking." He held up his hand to stop me from leaving and said, "Yes, I understand. I'll get right on it."

He took the referral form back from me, crumpled it, and tossed it into the trash can.

He called Ms. Rhodes, the receptionist, on the intercom and said, "Please let the staff know we will be dismissing students in one hour. And have Mrs. Parker send Tyler's backpack to the office. He'll be spending the rest of the morning in the office."

Mr. Dalton looked pretty calm, but it was evident that my weather prediction added another layer of irritation. I know I should stop while I am ahead, but I can't help myself. "Since we'll probably be out tomorrow, I'm sure the extra days off will help you."

"That's enough out of you, Tyler!" Mr. Dalton's voice no longer masked his irritation. "You know what, I think your lunch detention just increased to a two-day suspension. And if school is out tomorrow, you will serve it on Monday and Tuesday. I will call your mom as soon as all our students have been dismissed!"

"But why? I only made an honest statement based on how tired you look." My attempt to rationalize my words was useless. Mr. Dalton was mad and no longer hiding it. "Sorry," I added, peering out the office window. Snow flurries had begun to fall from the ominous clouds that, according to the weather radio in the office, now blanketed the entire state.

Two students from my class dropped off my backpack, and I took my usual seat in the waiting area. Mom will be so mad about the suspension. Our last family meeting, if you could call it that without Dad's presence, didn't go too well. Between the yelling and crying, I couldn't tell if Mom was having a nervous breakdown or if she just had enough of me.

The scene flashed in my mind as I was sitting there. Mom was already stressed enough about the house bills, and now she'll be upset about missing work for another suspension. I could hear her words playing in my head. *"My boss will not tolerate the constant calls from the school. You are making this so hard on me, and I don't have much patience left! Why are you doing this? What happened to my well-behaved little boy? Where did he go? I don't have the strength to do this much longer, Tyler!"*

Mom's last sentence repeated loudly in my thoughts, and suddenly I felt overwhelmed. No way will I let anyone see this. I asked Ms. Rhodes if I could go to the restroom. She gave me permission but said to use the restroom in the office. She added a little dig when she said to be sure to keep it tidy. Then she turned away to answer a ringing phone.

I hurried to the restroom before the tears could start. I closed the door and stood by the sink looking in the mirror. Why now? Why the tears? I'm sure I have become stronger over the last five months. I don't let anything or anyone bother me. I can't explain this sadness I'm feeling. I tell myself to stop these thoughts. Now isn't the time for this. There's a knock on the door. I quickly answered, "I'm in here," tucking away any sign of emotion.

"Hurry up, Tyler. We're about to load the buses," Mr. Dalton said.

"Okay, I'll be out in a minute."

Although I never used it, I flushed the toilet and then splashed water on my face. The chill from the water burned against my skin and helped chase away the ridiculous sadness trying to overtake me. After drying my face and hands, I unlocked the door, grabbed my backpack, and headed to my bus.

On the way, I made sure I didn't say a word to anyone, but I did catch glances from some of the students in my class. They really needed to mind their own business, but that's the problem with fifth graders. They aren't mature enough to mind their own business and leave everyone else alone.

CHAPTER 11

RANT OVER

LUCKILY, MY STOP WAS the second one on the afternoon bus route, so I didn't have to endure the curious glances for long. I have at least five hours before Mom gets home from work. I decided to take advantage of my temporary freedom and flopped on the couch and turned on the TV. As I flipped through the channels, most of the programs had been interrupted by emergency weather alerts. I settled on a rerun of *How It's Made*. Dad and I used to watch this together. We both have a natural curiosity for everyday stuff's inner workings, and this series satisfied our craving.

Fifteen minutes into the program, the sadness I tried to shake off earlier returned. I switched off the TV and decided to listen to music instead. Mom usually listened to Pop music on a streaming service, so I let her pre-selected station play. Taylor Swift's "Mean" started playing. I never really paid much attention to the lyrics until today. As she sang the chorus, one word hit me hard—mean.

For the first time, I realized that the song described the person I have become. Until now, I had never considered myself mean. I needed to protect myself from the meanness from others, from the disappointment they caused, that's all. But in the process, it's changing who I am. Over the last five months, I have built a hard shell around myself so nothing or no one can hurt me. Is it possible that I've gone too far? Before this school year, no one would consider me mean. Far from it. I loved school and enjoyed hanging out with my friends.

Until Dad started a new job at a prestigious law firm, we spent every summer exploring new trails and working on crazy inventions inspired by our favorite Discovery Channel series. Mom would capture videos and pictures of each stage, and we celebrated when the outcome was successful and laughed when it wasn't. Life was good back then. I drifted further into my thoughts but was brought back to reality when my phone rang. Mom was calling.

"Hi, Mom." I hoped she hadn't heard from Mr. Dalton yet.

"Tyler, are you home safely?"

"Yes, the bus dropped me off about an hour ago."

"Good. By the way, I had a call from Mr. Dalton."

"That was quick," I said without considering the intent of my words.

"Excuse me, that was quick. Is that all you can say?"

"No, Mom, that's not what I meant. Mr. Dalton seemed so distracted with the early dismissal I thought he might not call you until later." This conversation was not going well, and it probably was not going to get any better.

"A two-day suspension. Are you kidding me, Ty? After the last family meeting, I thought you got the message, but apparently nothing is sinking into your brain these days. I don't like the person you have become. I would never have thought my kind and considerate son would become a bully!"

"A bully?" I barely interrupted her rant.

"Yes, a bully! My sweet boy has become a bully, and I will not accept this. I planned to talk with you this weekend about some changes our family will make, but I think now is the best time. We are selling the house and moving to an apartment in a new town. We'll still be in the Portland area, but the schools will be different. The bills have gotten out of control, and so have you. It's time for a fresh start for both of us, and I expect things to change. Do you hear me?"

"Are you kidding? We're moving? Why? What if Dad comes back?" Like the ice-cold water in the office bathroom, her words stung my entire body. I felt numb, and a sick feeling hit my stomach.

"As much as I hate to admit it, Dad's not coming home, Tyler. Besides, we can't afford to stay in this house any longer, and your behavior, well, it's the last straw."

"But, Mom, you can't—"

"End of conversation, Tyler! It's happening, and we will spend the weekend and your two days of suspension packing and getting the house ready to be sold. I will be home by five. Make sure your homework is finished by the time I get there and no TV or music. Do you hear me?"

"Yeah."

"Excuse me!"

"Yes, ma'am."

"That's better." There was a brief pause then Mom said, "Ty, I really do love you, but things need to change. I'll see you soon. Start your homework now."

"Okay." I wanted to say be careful while driving home, but I'm too stunned by Mom's words to say anything more.

Moving? I don't want to move. Why is this happening? It's so unfair. What if Dad does come back? And I can't believe Mom called me a bully. A bully? Yeah, maybe I've become a little mean, but a bully . . . I'm not a bully. The more I thought about it, the more I disagreed with Mom's thinking.

I had dropped my backpack on the floor by the couch when I got home. I pulled out the chapter book Mrs. Parker assigned for us to read, but no matter how hard I tried to read the first chapter, I couldn't focus on anything but what Mom said. Why does she think I'm a bully? As I searched for the answer, my thoughts returned to the first day of fifth grade. I wasn't a bully before that, so somewhere between that first day of fifth grade and now, I turned into a different person. Have I become a bully?

CHAPTER 12

PACK IT AWAY IN A BOX

THE RATTLE OF THE rising garage door woke me from a sound sleep. I must have drifted off while thinking about all the events of the last five months that got me to where and who I am today.

Yes, I've changed, but I had no choice. I always hear grown-ups say that growing up is hard, and the decisions you make today will make you the person you will be six months from now. From where I stand, I am stronger today than I was six months ago. I no longer let others get the best of me. Instead, I shut them down before they have an opportunity to strike.

There's no such thing as a best friend. We convince ourselves that these friendships exist, but they're temporary. People are generally selfish, including parents. My dad has proved that time and time again these last few months and now my mom with her ridiculous declaration about moving. She never bothered to take time to get my opinion about it. Instead, she dropped it on me like a grenade. Boom! Life as I know it is obliterated. New home, new school, but somehow, I don't think anything will change with this fresh start.

By the time Mom came into the house from the garage, I was sitting at the kitchen table pretending to do homework. I quickly brushed my fingers through my hair, which had become matted from lying on the couch.

"Have you been working all afternoon?" Mom asked.

"Pretty much." I tried to sound convincing.

"That's good," she said as she stacked some groceries on the counter. "There's a stack of flattened boxes in the trunk for our move. Please unload them, and take five or six to your room to start packing. The packing tape should be on the floor of the passenger seat."

"So, it's happening?"

"Yes."

"Aren't we going to talk about it?" I asked this even though I could tell she was not in the mood.

"There's nothing to talk about. I've had a bad day and your suspension—well, let's say, it hasn't helped."

As Mom was putting away the last few groceries, her phone rang, so our conversation ended abruptly.

"Hello." After a brief pause she continued, "Yes, this is she." There was another pause. "No problem, your timing is perfect. I plan to have the house packed in about a week. Next Saturday will be perfect. What time can we expect you?" She motioned me to get a move on the boxes.

My body shuddered from the cold air as I reached into the trunk of Mom's car and grabbed the flattened boxes. The snow on the car was already melting, so I tried my best not to get the boxes wet. There were various sizes, so I stacked similar boxes in separate piles. Walking back for the final stack, a feeling of defeat overwhelmed me. How can this be happening? We're moving in just over a week, right in the middle of fifth grade. Why is Mom doing this to us? She's giving up too soon. I don't want to leave this house or my school. Yeah, school is not the best these days, but it's what I know. The unknown is scarier, at least to me. But why am I surprised? After all, life has become a series of disappointments, and this is another episode in my timeline.

I carried a load of flattened boxes to my room. It didn't take me long to put the boxes together, and they filled up quickly. It looks like I will need quite a few more, but this may be an ideal time to eliminate things that no longer matter. On the top shelf in my closet, I found all the Home STEM Challenge projects my dad and I worked on over the last few years. At the time, they were too good to trash, but now the memories are too emotionally hard to remember. I decided to put them in the trash pile. If I had the help of a few friends, my room would already be packed. But most of the friends I used to hang out with during the weekends are no longer worth my time. They ask too many questions, and I don't want anyone to know my business.

The grumbling in my stomach was dictating a snack break, and I needed more boxes anyway before I could pack anything else, so

I made my way downstairs. I poured cereal and milk into a large bowl, took a seat at the counter, and decided to complete some of the science homework I should have worked on earlier. I scanned the assignment sheet. Watch an *Animal Planet* segment and write five summary sentences. That sounded easy. I grabbed my laptop and started a search on YouTube.

Scanning through a dozen or so titles, I clicked on the third entry and began watching. A man with an Australian accent was talking about how animals have an instinct that helps them survive in times of danger. Whenever an animal feels pain or fear, it seeks safety. When an animal encounters fear, it typically experiences super strength, and its senses become sharper. The narrator called it self-preservation, and he said it's something that the animal kingdom has in common with humans.

The narrator's words replayed in my mind as I begin drifting back to my conversation with Mom on the phone earlier today. She called me a bully, but she's got it all wrong. My actions over the last five months are like those described by the narrator in this *Animal Planet* segment. Self-preservation is not bullying. Sure, I'll admit I'm meaner than I used to be, but a bully? How can Mom be so off-track? What I have been doing made sense to me now. Self-preservation and meanness go hand in hand. I stared at the stack of flattened boxes still in the kitchen. If only I could pack away the events and misunderstandings of the last six months in a box and leave them behind for someone else to deal with. Or better yet, dump them in the trash.

I refocused my thoughts on the assignment and continued listening to the narrator. Under my breath, I pretended to mimic his accent as I repeated his words.

"Are you still doing your homework or are you wasting time?" Mom asked as she walked into the kitchen.

"Still doing my homework," I mumbled and watched the clip again to buy myself more time.

NEW SCHOOL EQUALS NEW TEACHER

THE NEW APARTMENT IS cozy. At least that's how Mom described it. Grown-ups often use the word cozy when they describe a cramped space. Somehow they believe that using a positive adjective makes everything better. It doesn't. Just like moving to a friendly neighborhood and a newly remodeled school isn't going to improve my situation.

It's Monday, January 30th, and my first day at Fern Creek Elementary. We arrived at the school early, and Mom walked me to the school office. Behind a heavy plastic sheet, construction workers were finishing some plastering as teachers began arriving. A tall man with wavy hair greeted us at the office counter.

"Good morning, Ms. Miller. I'm Mr. Phillips, the Assistant Principal. I apologize for the mess. These guys have been working all night and should finish before the rest of the students arrive. Our remodeling project is almost complete. Just a few more months to go." Turning to me, he said, "So, you must be Tyler. Welcome to Fern Creek Elementary!"

"Yeah, I mean, yes, I'm Tyler." He seemed nice but a little too energetic for a Monday morning.

"We've been expecting you. Your teacher, Mrs. Granger, is already here, so let's take a quick walk to your new classroom, and I'll make the introductions."

"Thank you, Mr. Phillips," Mom said.

Mr. Phillips and Mom spent the entire walk discussing the renovations happening at the school. He stopped several times to point out all the new additions to the building. Mom seemed interested, but I couldn't get into it. We made our way to the second floor. At the top of the stairs, I noticed a quote that read, "You are not better than anyone, but no one is better than you."

"What an interesting quote," Mom said, looking at me.

"Yeah, I guess."

"I'm glad you noticed that quote. It's one of my favorites. We added it a few years ago when we began the RAK Initiative project," Mr. Phillips said.

"RACK?" Mom asked, trying to guess the acronym.

"R – A – K. It stands for random acts of kindness. Here at Fern Creek we aspire to be a bully-free school and promote random acts of kindness as part of our school's natural culture," Mr. Phillips said, grinning from ear to ear.

In my opinion, he was too excited about the RAK thing, and I hoped it was just because my mom was here.

"That's wonderful! Don't you agree, Ty?" Mom said, giving me a cheeky grin.

I mimicked her grin and responded, "Sure," trying not to sound too sarcastic.

"I would love to tell you more, but I need to greet the buses in about five minutes. Let me introduce you to Mrs. Granger before I head to the buses."

"Oh, I'm sorry for taking up so much of your time, Mr. Phillips," Mom said.

"No need to apologize. Our principal, Mrs. Grant, is meeting with the construction foreman this morning, so I'm flying solo. Mrs. Grant usually walks the new students to class, so I'm glad I had the opportunity to meet Tyler, or do you prefer Ty?"

"Either is fine," I said, trying not to be rude.

"Then Ty it is! My younger brother also goes by Ty, so it will be easy for me to remember."

"Cool." Mr. Phillips was definitely friendlier than Mr. Dalton had been over the last few months.

"Here we are. Mrs. Granger, room 207."

Just above Mrs. Granger's name there was another quote. This one read, "Courage is fire, and bullying is smoke." I wondered what that was supposed to mean as I entered the room.

"Mrs. Granger, let me introduce you to Tyler Miller, your new student, and his mom, Ms. Miller."

Mrs. Granger looked nothing like Mrs. Parker. She is older, but probably not as old as my grandmother. She is wearing gold-rimmed glasses, and she has a crooked smile.

"Welcome, Ms. Miller and Tyler. It's a pleasure to meet you. Tyler, you're my third new student in the last few weeks. Which school did you attend before arriving here?"

"Woodland Park Elementary," I said, hoping to keep the conversation to a minimum.

"Isn't that a funny coincidence? One of my other new students also came from Woodland Park Elementary. You may know him. His name is Miguel Garcia-Molina. Do you recognize his name?" Mrs. Granger asked as she walked over to an empty desk and placed a name tag on the top right edge.

"Yeah—I mean, yes, I know him. I knew he left Woodland Park, but I didn't realize he transferred to Fern Creek," I said, wishing it wasn't true. Unlike me, Miguel was an actual bully and had been for years. He was in Ms. Tyson's fifth grade class, and even though I never hung out with Miguel, his reputation spoke for him. I can't believe we will be in the same class. I don't have a good feeling about this, but I'm not sure what I can do about it now.

"Actually, he went to Dogwood Trails Elementary for several weeks before transferring to Fern Creek Elementary. The builder was delayed in completing his family's new home, so they stayed with relatives until it was finished. With all the new housing construction surrounding our school, we have an uptick in new students. Was Miguel in your class at Woodland?" she asked.

"No, he was in Ms. Tyson's class, and I was in Mrs. Parker's class. I believe Miguel was in my kindergarten class, but we've been in different classes ever since," I explained.

"At least you'll be familiar with one student. That's a great way to start the first day at a new school." She handed my mom a folder and continued, "Ms. Miller, this folder has a copy of the school's handbook and our class schedule, along with some handouts for you to complete and return to me."

"Thank you, Mrs. Granger. I will look over the materials and return any paperwork tomorrow with Ty," Mom said, as she brushed a few strands of hair off my face.

"Mom, please stop." I tried to keep my voice down. I hated when she did this to me. It made me feel like a little kid, and it was embarrassing in front of my new teacher. Fortunately, Mrs. Granger's attention was on relocating my desk.

"I think I'll move your desk next to Miguel for today," she said.

"Mrs. Granger, you don't have to move my desk. I'm fine to sit where you already had it," I said, hoping she would move the desk back to its original spot.

"Oh, it's no bother. I want you to feel comfortable on your first day."

"Really, I'm fine to sit anywhere," I added, but my words did not seem to make a difference.

"It's done, so let's leave it next to Miguel for now."

"Thank you for making Ty feel welcome, Mrs. Granger," Mom said.

"Of course! The first day in a new school is always awkward. Glad I can help make it easier."

Unknowingly, Mrs. Granger made this day harder when she moved my desk next to Miguel's. I hope I am wrong, but I don't think so.

MORNING MEETING

ONCE THE BELL RANG it didn't take long for the other students to fill the room. A steady but controlled murmur grew within the classroom, but it didn't seem to interrupt Mrs. Granger's concentration. Her desk was cluttered with books and notepads, but she seemed to know exactly where everything was located. From the corner of my eye, I saw Miguel and another student enter the classroom. Instantly, the murmuring ceased, and all that could be heard was the exchange of dialogue between the two boys.

"Did you see her face?" the other kid asked.

"Yep! Redder than a hot pepper!" Miguel answered.

Both of them were laughing when Mrs. Granger interrupted them and said, "Good morning, boys!"

Miguel gave her a smirk, and said, "Good morning, Granger."

"It's Mrs. Granger to you, Mr. Garcia-Molina. I should not have to remind you each week."

"He's very sorry, Mrs. Granger," said the other kid in a snarky tone.

"Yeah, like he said!" Miguel added, and the two started laughing again.

"Let's remember for the future. Besides, there's someone here you may know, Miguel," she said.

"Who?"

"Tyler Miller. He was a student at Woodland Park Elementary."

"The 'Ty Miller' is here?" Miguel asked as I watched him look around the room.

"Yes, and he'll be sitting beside you," Mrs. Granger said.

"Sweet! The renegade of Woodland Park joins us at Fern Creek," Miguel said as he spied me sitting at my desk. "Ty, welcome to Fern

Creek! This here is Cameron." Miguel raised his hand to his forehead and saluted me. Cameron followed suit.

Renegade? What was that supposed to mean? From what I could tell, nothing had changed with Miguel, and his new side-kick, Cameron, didn't seem any better. Why did my mom think that moving to a new apartment and new school would fix everything? Leave it to adults to really mess things up!

"Yo, Ty! This is going to be epic." Miguel dumped his book bag on my desk, knocking over my water bottle.

"Oops, my bad!"

"No problem," I said, trying to soak up the spill with the sleeve of my jacket.

The final bell rang, and Mrs. Granger made her way to the stool at the front of the classroom.

"Good morning, class. I hope you enjoyed the weekend and are ready to start a new week of learning. Tyler Miller, a former Woodland Park Beaver, has joined our class this morning. Please make him feel welcome."

In unison, the entire class said, "Welcome, Tyler!" I tightened my jaw and acknowledged the welcome with a quick upward head nod. I didn't feel like talking with all eyes on me.

Mrs. Granger pulled up the projector screen to reveal a message on the board and said, "Take a moment to read this quote to yourself and think about its meaning."

I tried to shake off the greeting and refocus my attention on the quote neatly written on the board. I read the sentences several times. "Remember, there's no such thing as a small act of kindness. Every act creates a ripple with no logical end." Apparently, somebody named Scott Adams said this. Hmm, this must be part of that RAK Initiative program Mr. Phillips told Mom about.

"Is there anyone willing to share a connection you can make with this quote?" Mrs. Granger asked. A few hands went up. "Let's see . . . okay, Maddy, what is your connection?" she asks.

"When I read this quote, it makes me think of my family's trip to the lake last summer."

Her voice was so high-pitched and squeaky I couldn't help but laugh when Miguel raised his eyebrows and crinkled his nose like he was in pain. I mimicked his face right back, resulting in another laugh, this time from Miguel. Mrs. Granger looked in our direction and for several seconds she didn't say a word.

"Is there something funny, boys?"

All eyes are on me again, so I have no choice but to think of a clever response. "Well, kind of . . . I thought Maddy said her family tripped on a rake. I mean, it's not funny if they tripped on a rake, but when I realized I heard wrong, it made me laugh. When I laughed, it made Miguel laugh too. Sorry."

"I see. Well, please try to listen more carefully so that you don't misunderstand again. Please continue, Maddy. I can't wait to hear the rest of your thoughts."

"Like I said, when we visited the lake, my dad and I threw small pebbles along the water's surface to see who could create the longest ripple. No matter how hard I tried, his ripples were always longer than mine. Dad told me that even though it looked like a ripple ended, it actually still continued for a while, even when we could no longer see it."

Maddy paused several seconds after I made a barely audible snicker. I tried my best to hold in the laughter, even though it was extremely hard. Her voice—wow, I've never heard anything like it! I decided to bury my face in the fold of my elbow, which helped.

Maddy sighed and looked back at Mrs.

Granger before continuing. "Oh yeah, and the ripples can change directions as they travel! At least that's what my dad said. He's sort of a science geek. So, I guess when we perform an act of kindness, it creates a ripple, and its effect keeps going even when we can't see it."

"Maddy, that's a brilliant connection! Thank you for sharing," Mrs. Granger said, looking once more in my direction as if to say I expected better from you.

As Mrs. Granger continued with the morning meeting, Miguel mimicked the look she gave me, and I buried my face in my elbow again to avoid laughing. Miguel was hilarious and, from what I can now tell, someone who will be a good friend.

THREE AMIGOS

FOR THE MOST PART, the past five weeks flew by quickly. After a few rough spots, I finally felt settled at Fern Creek Elementary. Sure, I have given Mrs. Granger the occasional hiccup, and I got banned from standing or sitting near Cameron and Miguel or even looking at them in class. Regardless, the three of us have become solid friends. Miguel's mom nicknamed us the three amigos, and I kind of liked it, especially when she said it with her Latin accent. Indeed, the three of us are great friends. We think alike, laugh at the same things, and see life from a similar perspective. We had perfected "self-preservation," even though some adults continued to call it "bullying." It was interesting how everyone was a bully nowadays. It was definitely an overused word, at least in my opinion.

When I started riding the bus, I was surprised to see Cameron and Miguel load the bus two stops after mine. Sweet. Cameron suggested we keep it chill on the bus so our driver, Ms. Whipple, would not separate us. So far, so good. I kept a notebook in my backpack that we passed back and forth. That's how we communicated, and we have managed to stay out of trouble.

I safeguarded the notebook to keep it from making its way into the wrong hands. Since so many people were overly sensitive these days, a few outside readers might consider our scribbles inappropriate. We just comment on what we see. If people were honest, they would agree with our statements. Take Maddy's voice. It's deadly, to put it mildly. Mr. Minotti, another bus driver, sounds like Harry, the shorter of the two bandits from the *Home Alone* movies. His thick, New York accent sticks out like a sore thumb in these parts. Seriously Simon— yep, that's his nickname—is the biggest science geek in my class. He is obsessed with dinosaurs, and no matter what we're discussing in class, he can always hijack the conversation and insert some obnoxious dinosaur factoid. He's so weird. I found myself laughing and walking the opposite direction whenever I saw him coming. And there's this girl named Ella in Mr. Bailey's fifth grade class. She acts as if her dog died or something along those lines. She never smiles. Maybe she behaves differently inside her classroom, but I doubt it. Whatever her problem is, she carries it everywhere she goes. What a loser!

It was Monday again and the start of another week at Fern Creek Elementary. Spring break was getting closer, and Mrs. Grant kept talking about the big cleanup project. The renovations were nearly complete, and although the custodians worked really hard to keep the school clean, debris and dust from the construction had settled into every crevice of the building, both the new and the old. Mrs. Grant was a dreamer. She believed everyone—parents, students, and staff—would give up one or two days of their spring break to volunteer for clean-up at the school until every part sparkled. Maybe it will happen; perhaps it won't. Miguel, Cameron, and I don't plan to volunteer. After the year I've had, I need a break. Besides, the three amigos have big plans, and nothing will stop us from seeing them through.

CHAPTER 16

Early March

A VISIT WITH MRS. RUSSELL

ON A GLOOMY TUESDAY in early March, Mrs. Russell, the school counselor, entered our classroom with a basket of materials. She walked over to Mrs. Granger and spoke quietly with her before moving to the front of the room.

"Good morning, Mrs. Granger's fifth graders. I'm going to spend the next forty-five minutes with you. Please clear your desk and take out a pencil," Mrs. Russell said, giving us a warm smile as we complied.

I looked over at Miguel and rolled my eyes. Obviously, we would be spending the next forty-five minutes talking about bullying. Bullying is definitely a buzzword these days. Why can't adults let this go? This school is obsessed with anti-bullying talks. They act as if everyone is a bully or is bullied. Life in the twenty-first century is survival of the fittest like we learned in science. Sure, I agree that the world needs more kindness, but have you met some of the people out there? They don't know when to mind their own business. There are many "Jacksons" out there who always need to be right and make everyone else feel small. I'm not letting anyone make me feel small. Putting them in their place before they attack, well, that's the best way to keep them out of your personal business.

I cleared my desk as directed and took out a pencil. Mrs. Russell had her materials spread out on top of an empty desk.

"I would like to take about ten minutes to read you a story before I have you complete a task. The title of this book is *The Invisible Boy* written by Trudy Ludwig. Before I begin, does anyone want to predict the central message of this story?" Mrs. Russell asked, scanning the room for volunteers.

Without thinking, I raised my hand but immediately put it down.

"Mr. Miller, thank you for raising your hand," Mrs. Russell said.

"Uh, I was stretching," I said, hoping she would move on.

"Oh, come on, Mr. Miller. I'm sure you can make a prediction. Why not give it a go?" Mrs. Russell said as she made an empty desktop her seat.

Everyone was now looking in my direction, and I could feel my face begin to burn from embarrassment. The phrase "self-preservation" streamed through my thoughts on repeat mode.

I didn't want to do this, especially since everyone was looking and already passing judgment on my answer even before I spoke a word. That's how kids are nowadays. I decided to go for a laugh. "I think the central message of this story is don't be a loser or you'll become invisible."

Miguel, Cameron, and several others snickered at my answer, but my words did not impress Mrs. Russell. She did her best to hide her frustration.

"Not quite the direction I hoped you would take, Mr. Miller."

"Sorry." I paused and continued, "As I said, I didn't mean to raise my hand. You should have called on someone else, like Maddy. She loves to hear herself talk." In hindsight, I should have left the last part out.

"Mr. Miller, you owe Maddy an apology. I expect better from you and this class."

"Sorry, Maddy." Once again, the stares from the entire class made me uncomfortable, and self-preservation took over. Turning toward Maddy, I added, "You have to admit I'm right. No one else in this room likes to talk more than you. It's just the truth." Maddy stared back at me in disbelief as her eyes welled up with tears.

"Mr. Miller!" Mrs. Russell stood up, took a deep breath, and said, "Please step outside with me." There was a quiver in her voice, and I knew she was not happy.

I mustered the courage to get up from my desk and walk across the room. I pushed down the embarrassment that was trying to creep up. I'll get a lecture, and then Mrs. Russell will forget the incident. That's how she rolls. Mrs. Russell followed behind me and closed the door before speaking.

"Tyler, your behavior was highly inappropriate and disappointing on so many levels. I've decided to add you to the anti-bullying group that meets three times a week."

"Anti-bullying? Are you kidding? Why?" I asked.

"If you need me to tell you why, then you obviously need to be in the group. I have a lesson to complete. Please go next door and wait in Mrs. Handler's classroom. I will come and get you when I finish. And while you're there, please read this."

She handed me a copy of *The Invisible Boy*, and I made my way to Mrs. Handler's room.

CHAPTER 17

HOORAY FOR THE ANTI-BULLYING GROUP . . . NOT!

MRS. RUSSELL DID NOT waste any time. Before leaving my classroom, she scheduled me to be part of the anti-bullying group. And, of course, Mrs. Granger was more than willing to oblige her decision.

Maybe I had taken my actions too far, but I basically had no choice. I don't like being embarrassed just as much as I don't want people knowing my business. Now, without my consent, I am a member of the anti-bullying group. Hooray, for me. Yeah, not so much! I think the best way to survive the torture is to keep my ears open and my mouth shut. I'll give the occasional nod or positive expression, which should suffice. Mrs. Russell isn't too pushy.

Hmm, I bet there will be questions—lots of questions. How will I handle the questions? Think, Ty . . . think. Got it. If I repeat or, better yet, restate what everyone else says, that should buy me time, and before long, the group meetings will be over. I don't even have to agree with the words I mimic. It's all a game of survival, and now I have a viable plan before I'm thrown into the fire. Another win for self-preservation!

SPRING BREAK SURPRISE

MY PLAN WORKED. I came through the anti-bullying group unscathed and unchanged. Determination and saying what adults want to hear, that's how it's done! Spring break was finally here. Mom agreed to volunteer for several days, and I agreed not to get in her way. After all, Cameron, Miguel, and I have plans for each day of the week. It will be epic and more fun than I have had since moving to this new town.

"Are you sure you don't mind that I'm volunteering at the school today?" Mom asked as I was sitting at the kitchen table eating my breakfast.

"Nope, I've got plans with Cameron and Miguel. We confirmed last night."

"Are you sure you don't want to come with me, even for a few hours?"

"No, I'm good. I need a break from school. We agreed last week."

"Yes, I know. I just thought you might change your mind if you knew your dad was going to be there."

"Huh? Did you say Dad is volunteering at Fern Creek?"

"Yes, you heard right. Your dad is going to be there today. He texted me late last night."

"How did he even know about the clean-up at the school?"

"He read it in the principal's newsletter."

"I'm confused. How did Dad get the principal's newsletter? It's not in his DNA to look things up on the school's website."

"You're spot on, but he didn't have to look for it. The newsletter came to his Inbox. He's listed as a contact on your registration and receives all the announcements and emails from the school each week."

"Duh, I guess he is my dad. It's been so long since I've seen him, I almost forgot."

"I know, and I'm sorry. Your dad's new

job consumes all his time—at least that's what he said in the text."

"Mom, do you believe he's really going to show up?"

"You know, I've had my doubts this year, but I believe he's going to be there. So, are you going to change your mind about joining me?"

"Uhm . . . okay. I better text Cameron and Miguel and let them know I'll need to postpone our plans for today."

"Sounds like a good idea. I've already laid out your work clothes in the laundry room. Get changed while I pack us a lunch. Ham or turkey?" Mom asked as she opened the fridge.

"Ham with shredded lettuce. And do we have any kettle chips?"

"Yep! You may look like your dad, but you've got my quirky eating habits. Ham, lettuce, and kettle chips smashed together inside a multigrain roll."

"The best!"

It didn't take me long to change clothes and text my friends who were unhappy that plans were changing. They'll get over it. Besides, we have all week to be together. I grabbed Dad's patrol cap from my closet and put it on. I stopped to take a quick look in the mirror. Not bad, even if I do say so myself. It would be great if Dad wore his cap that he should have worn on Halloween. It was wishful thinking, but that would be the icing on the cake. I made my way to the car to wait for Mom. Maybe today will be the start of better days ahead. I am hopeful, but time will tell. It always does.

CHAPTER 19

IT'S A SMALL WORLD

AS MOM PULLED INTO the school's parking lot, I looked for Dad's car. It's strange that when you start to look for a particular car model, suddenly you see it everywhere. Dad drives a blue Honda Civic Hatchback. I spotted several of them in the parking lot, but I didn't see Dad's car. His Civic proudly displays the bumper stickers "Army Strong" and "Be All You Can Be." There are already a ton of cars at the school, which is surprising, especially since it's the first day of spring break.

"I believe that's your dad talking to Mr. Phillips outside the front office," Mom said as she pulled into an open spot.

"Huh? Where?"

"Just beside the plaque outside the front office."

"It is Dad, and he's wearing his patrol cap!"

"That's how I spotted him," Mom said as she parked the car and turned off the engine. "Grab the cooler in the trunk before you run off."

"Sure! Do you think we can work in the same area?"

"I'm sure we can arrange that with Mrs. Grant. I emailed her first thing this morning."

"You're the best, Mom! Thank you. I'll grab the cooler and then go see Dad."

Dad and Mr. Phillips appeared to be having a good conversation. Dad was smiling, and so was Mr. Phillips.

"Hey, big guy! How amazing is this—we both wore our caps!" Dad said, giving me a high five.

"Yeah, I thought I'd take the chance just in case you had the same idea."

"I guess great minds think alike!" added Mr. Phillips, giving me a wink. "I've been talking with your dad, Ty. My older brother, Nathan, served in the Army in the same company as your dad. It's a small world!"

"Wow, that's cool! Do you remember him, Dad?"

"I sure do. Nate the Great, that's what we called him. A great guy and soldier. Nate never met a stranger. Probably one of the kindest guys you will ever meet," Dad said as Mom made her way toward us.

"Yeah, I didn't always appreciate that about him back then, but I sure do now," Mr. Phillips said, putting his hand out to greet Mom.

"Hello, Mr. Phillips. It's great to see you. It looks like Mrs. Grant's clean-up campaign will be a great success," Mom said as she smiled at Dad.

"Mrs. Grant is an organizational master and marketing whiz. She secured volunteers from many of our vendors and construction crew. Her idea to purchase hard hats that matched her outfits has made her a standout with the community. They love her, and for a good reason. The *Portland Observer* is publishing an article about her," Mr. Phillips said.

"I've taken note of her different hardhats. Her collection is quite remarkable," Mom said.

"Ty, I'm so glad you are here with your parents. Several food trucks should arrive around eleven. My favorite is Kee's Loaded Kitchen. Her sweet and salty fried chicken and saucy mac and cheese are brilliant!" Mr. Phillips said.

"I'm hungry already," Dad said, giving me a wink. "Thanks, Mr. Phillips! Let's get this party started. What do you two think?"

"That's what we're here to do!" Mom answered.

"Let me see here . . ." Mr. Phillips muttered, looking down at his clipboard. "It looks like you've been assigned to the new gymnasium. Ty, why don't you take your parents to the gym and look for Coach Mulligan? He'll show you what needs to be done."

"Sure will, Mr. Phillips." The gym is the perfect spot for my family. Dad is all about sports.

As the three of us walked to the gymnasium, I couldn't help but feel happy. Dad was here with us, and for the first time in a long while, he hadn't backed out. I really wanted to believe that it would be like this from now on, but I don't want to get my hopes up. My birthday is coming up soon, and all I want is to spend time with Dad. That will be the only gift I need. But for now, I'm going to focus on today. Today is as close to perfect as it can be.

A GOOD DISTRACTION

SPRING BREAK WAS REASONABLY decent. Dad spent the entire day with us for the school clean-up day and then took us to dinner at my favorite Japanese Hibachi grill. Mom smiled the whole time, and for a brief moment, we were a family again.

I missed the days when I didn't have to worry about my parents splitting up. Honestly, I still don't get it. Why can't they see how happy they both look when they're around each other? Dad was always a lawyer, but suddenly, with a new job, my parents didn't want to be a family any longer. I overheard Mom talking to

Grandma Sato the other night, and she mentioned divorce several times! The whole thing doesn't make sense to me. Adults are hard to understand at times, but kids can be just as complicated, I guess.

Mrs. Granger was dressed differently this morning, and everyone was wondering why. It didn't take long before she explained her appearance.

"Today, we begin our preparation for the annual fifth grade kickball tournament, scheduled in mid-May. Mr. Bailey's class has taken the title for the last two years, although my former fifth grade students gave his class a run for their money. We almost won last year, and I know we can win this year. It's our year. I can feel it in my bones."

Mrs. Granger sounded serious about winning the kickball tournament, and I'm on board. There's no way the other classes can beat us. Mrs. Hansen's class is seriously a most non-athletic group of individuals, and so is Ms. Lawson's class. Sure, Mr. Bailey has a few good athletes like Thomas and Blake, but that's pretty much it. I don't know much about Mrs. Handler's class, but they seem more artsy than athletic. Students in her class created most of the artwork in the fifth grade hallway. Mrs. Rossi's thick Brooklyn accent is scary, but her class is not intimidating. She has several tall girls and a few boys who play travel ball, but that doesn't automatically make them great at kickball. Yeah, we've got this. I'm ninety-nine percent sure of it.

"Let's begin our morning meeting. Take a minute to read the quote on the board before we start our discussion," Mrs. Granger said.

I began to read the words from Maya Angelou neatly printed on the board. "I've learned that people will forget what you said, people will forget what you did, but people will never forget how you made them feel."

My thoughts shift to the individuals who have made my life difficult over the last ten months. Hopefully, I made them feel bad for not minding their own business, and they've learned their lesson. Self-preservation was not easy, but it was necessary to survive in today's world.

Mrs. Granger moved to the back of the room before asking, "How do you think a person feels after receiving a random act of kindness?"

I knew it. Everything at this school

revolves around kindness. It's funny how some still have not learned to mind their own business. Their words and actions get under my skin, and I can't help but shut them down. Random acts of kindness interfere with an individual's personal space. In my opinion, I'm expressing kindness by minding my own business and maintaining boundaries. My thoughts drifted back to spring break and the fantastic day Mom and I spent with Dad. Although it took ten days before I heard Dad's voice again, his communication has improved.

During our last phone conversation, we exchanged small talk for the first fifteen minutes, and then the best part came. Dad promised to take me camping on my birthday weekend. The last time Dad and I did something together alone was in late June when we spent a whole afternoon mapping out the white water rafting details for the trip that never happened. I wanted to be excited about the potential camping trip, but what if history repeated itself? I can't face another letdown. It's too much to juggle for an almost eleven-year-old kid. Do I tell Cameron and Miguel about our plans, or should I keep the details to myself? Can I trust Dad to keep his promise? I wanted to believe it with everything in me, but the part of me that trusts is permanently damaged. It's still a while before my birthday, so anything could happen to mess up the plans.

Mrs. Granger walked toward my group and stopped a few feet from my desk. "Mr. Miller, any thoughts on the quote?"

I scrambled to reread the quote then realized Mrs. Granger might not appreciate my viewpoint. "No, I'm good. But I do need to use the restroom."

"You should have gone before class started. Make it quick!"

"Will do!" I didn't waste any time, and was out of the door within seconds. Once in the hall, I slowed my pace. I needed to be out just long enough to avoid the rest of the morning meeting. It's best to keep my interactions to a minimum. Less contact means less drama, and I'm all for that.

GUM, KICKBALL, AND A REAL LOSER

KEEPING THE BIRTHDAY CAMPING trip a secret was harder than I had anticipated. The first time Miguel, Cameron, and I hung out after school, I spilled the beans. They promised not to say anything about it at school, and since our class spent many recesses practicing for the kickball tournament, the conversation never came up.

Today is April 16th, and our class had a free recess day so two other classes could use the fields for kickball practice. Cameron, Miguel, and I decided to watch our competition. Mrs. Rossi's class was on the field closest to the gym. After watching for several minutes, I determined that her class was not our competition. The girls that played travel ball were so full of themselves. Mrs. Rossi put them in charge. Big mistake! Her class spent a lot of time stretching, and when they finally started playing, no one knew what to do. It was good for a laugh.

"Let's check out Mr. Bailey's class. After all, they are the class to beat," said Cameron.

"Good idea," I said, sneaking a piece of gum into my mouth.

"Hey, aren't you going to share?" Miguel asked.

"Yeah, but don't blow it for me!"

"Whatever! Mrs. Granger is too far away to notice. I'll swallow it before we line up," Miguel answered.

"Why swallow it? I press it up against my molars and then continue chewing after school," Cameron boasted.

"That's because you're a loser!" I say, giving Miguel a fist bump.

"Nah! I'm just smarter than the two of you," Cameron said, snatching two pieces of gum from my hand.

"Hey! Why did you take two?"

"Because you called me a loser. Who's the loser now?" Cameron asked, smirking from ear to ear.

"Hey, who is that kid?" I asked, pointing toward home plate.

"It's a new student. I saw Mrs. Grant walk him to Mr. Bailey's class this morning," Miguel said.

"He looks like a fish out of water! What's wrong with him?" asked Cameron.

I watched him for a minute. "They're all cheering for him, but I don't think that will help."

"He looks scared of the ball. And he's going for it . . ." Miguel laughed. "Oh, snap! Did you see that?" Cameron shook his head in disbelief.

"Yep, sure did! And the new kid trips over the ball, ladies and gentlemen! Pandemonium fills the playground at Fern Creek Elementary! And our star player is out for the count!" shouted Miguel, in his best announcer voice.

"No way! He didn't trip. That kid just passed out! What a loser!" My mind cannot comprehend the wimpiness displayed right in front of us. I started laughing uncontrollably, and Miguel and Cameron followed suit. Mr. Bailey's class doesn't have a chance with this loser, although Blake, Thomas, and that depressed girl Ella are surprisingly solid players. Returning my thoughts to the new kid, it was too bad I didn't have a video of the big faint. That was meme-worthy material! Just when I think my laughter is under control, Cameron's wad of gum flew out of his mouth mid-laugh, and we all lost it again!

"I guess you're not going to be chewing that piece of gum after school!" Miguel snickered in between bouts of laughter.

Some of Mr. Bailey's students looked over at us, but we didn't stop laughing. Without thinking, I repeated, "What a loser," while pointing toward the new kid. This kid named Andre or Andy gave me a disapproving look. Oh, well. He'll get over it! If he saw what we saw, he'd be laughing too!

A LECTURE, A QUOTE, AND THE UNEXPECTED PASSENGER

SOMEHOW MRS. GRANGER CAUGHT wind of our playground antics, and after a brief one-sided conversation about her deep disapproval of our behavior, we walked back into the classroom and found our seats. After fussing at her desk for several minutes, Mrs. Granger walked to the front of the room carrying her book of kindness quotes. Here we go again!

"Thank you for your patience, boys and girls. I had a few issues to address, but now we will continue with our afternoon. Before we begin the science lesson, I would like to share a quote by Franklin D. Roosevelt. He said, "Human kindness has never weakened the stamina or softened the figure of a free people. A nation does not have to be cruel to be tough." Does anyone have any thoughts or comments about this quote?" she asked, scanning the room for partakers.

After what felt like an eternity, a few hands popped up. Mrs. Granger smiled and looked over at Maddy. Oh no, please don't pick her, I thought. I knew I couldn't hold back the laughter today. Luckily, Mrs. Granger called on Laynie.

"This quote is more challenging than the others you have shared, Mrs. Granger, but I think I have a comment," she said, sitting up a bit taller.

"Yes, I agree. It's definitely more thought-provoking, but I feel it fits well for today. Go ahead, Laynie."

"Well, I think Franklin D. Roosevelt . . . wait, was he a president?" she asked.

"Yes, that is correct, Laynie. Franklin D. Roosevelt was the thirty-second president of the United States and won a record four elections. Sometimes people refer to him as FDR."

"I've heard that before. Thanks, Mrs. Granger. Anyway, I believe Mr. Roosevelt, or

FDR, wanted us to know that people or a nation can be powerful and still act kindly. Kindness is not a weakness. It is a strength."

"Laynie, you are a superstar! Your thoughts are spot-on! It is much harder to be kind than it is to be cruel. It takes great strength to lead by kindness. I hope we can remember this truth as we complete the last few months of fifth grade. Now, let's get back to science. Team leaders, please grab your materials for our experiment."

Throughout the entire science activity, my thoughts drifted back to recess. Sure, Mrs. Granger wasn't thrilled with our behavior, and we had to endure another kindness quote, but there was no denying it. That new kid is the biggest loser I've seen in a while.

The afternoon passed quickly, and before too long, Cameron, Miguel, and I boarded bus 284. All was status quo until I saw the new kid walking down the aisle. Are you kidding? Apparently, we are privileged to ride with the biggest loser at Fern Creek Elementary.

"Look who's walking our way," I said, giving Cameron a nudge.

"The loser is avoiding eye contact. Good call, J.R., or whatever your name is," Miguel said.

"I think his class called him R.J., not J.R.," Cameron corrected, causing us to laugh.

Upon hearing our laughter, Ms. Whipple, the bus driver, looked in her rearview mirror and gave us a disapproving look. The three of us gave her a thumbs up, and we quickly reverted to using the notebook. We decided to recreate the entire fainting incident using funny dialogue, and no matter how hard we tried, the occasional fit of laughter sneaked out. Ms. Whipple's focus had moved on to a few younger students who spilled Cheetos all over the floor, so we were in the clear.

Occasionally, I looked over at R.J. to check out what he was doing. His body language told me he knew we were talking about him. He looked sad and pathetic. A loser to the core and not someone I wanted as a friend.

When we arrived at my stop, the three of us got off. Mom was okay with us playing Xbox while she was at work. It took a week to convince her. When Dad didn't call on Saturday, she caved. It will be awesome as Miguel brought a new game we've wanted to play for weeks.

R.J. was still sulking in his seat as the bus pulled away. A time I felt the same way flashed across my mind, but I quickly shook it off. I was pathetic for a brief time. Not my proudest moment. I know better now, and nothing or no one will make me feel like that again. In fact, when I replayed R.J.'s unfortunate fainting spell in my mind, I couldn't help but laugh. Laughing makes me feel good, and that's what counts. After all, I need to think about number one. In this case, it's me.

MR. PHILLIPS

R.J. DIDN'T RIDE THE bus again after his infamous first day. Wow, that kid needed to get some tougher skin or his life would be miserable, especially in middle school. He needed to learn the art of self-preservation. I've mastered it! Honestly, I don't know why I even care. I don't know him, and from what I've seen, I don't care to know him. Jennilee, Sophie, and Andy, some students in Mr. Bailey's class, have been hanging out with him, so I guess that qualified them to be members of the loser club.

It was Friday morning and another school week was almost over! As Miguel, Cameron, and I entered the school building from the bus lot, Jennilee, Sophie, and Andy were front and center blocking our path. A coincidence maybe, but my natural curiosity took over.

"Where's your loser friend?" I asked.

"Are you talking to us?" asked Jennilee.

"Yeah, are you deaf?" asked Miguel, giving Cameron a satisfying high-five.

"No, we heard you. You never talk to us, so why now?" Andy asked while the two girls moved closer to him.

"Actually, we have no interest in talking with you guys. You were in our way, so I asked a question in the hope that you'd scatter and get out of our space. But, since we have your attention, let me offer you some advice. Stay away from R.J. Any kid afraid of a harmless kickball is a pathetic loser. And by hanging out with him, you become losers by association. It's that simple. You've wasted enough of our morning, so that's all I have to say."

The three of us walked away, smiling. For some reason, after a rocky start at home this morning, those words felt satisfying to me. Cameron and Miguel never noticed when something was bothering me. They just expected me to be tough, and I always delivered.

The first hour of school was pretty uneventful. We started the day with another kindness quote by some do-gooder named Bob Kerrey. "Unexpected kindness is the most powerful, least costly, and most underrated agent of human change." Mrs. Granger spent most of the morning meeting discussing the quote. The majority of the class was fully engaged, giving positive example after positive example. But I found myself thinking that kindness took more energy and more time than I was willing to give. It was not my place to change anyone. I've got enough on my plate.

Just as we were about to transition into reading, Mr. Phillips walked into our classroom straight to Mrs. Granger without greeting the class. They exchanged whispers for approximately thirty seconds before Mr. Phillips motioned to Cameron, Miguel, and me to follow him.

It's going to be another beautiful day in the neighborhood. Not! Mr. Rogers lied, but he had one thing right. We all live in the neighborhood of make-believe. Yep, nothing is real and the people are fake. Mr. Phillips did not say a word the entire walk to his office. I noticed an uneasiness come over Cameron and

Miguel. When push came to shove, they were lightweights. I guess that's why I take the lead in this friendship.

"I will speak with Cameron and Miguel first. You can sit there, and I will call for you when I am ready," Mr. Phillips said to me, pointing to the chair in the farthest corner.

"Got it." I walked over to take a seat.

I sat and waited. Nothing new to me. I've done this before. When it was my turn to see Mr. Phillips, I realized right away that he meant business. The banter we shared during spring break was gone. His tone was serious, and I was pretty sure this meeting was not going to end well.

"Tyler, this morning I received a bully report. You and your two friends were named; however, it appears that you were the instigator."

"Mr. Phillips, I may be many things, but I am not a bully, at least not in the full sense of the word."

"In the full sense? What is that supposed to mean?"

"Well, bullying has no purpose. I practice self-preservation. After all, if I don't look out for number one, no one will."

"I hate to break it to you, Tyler, but you are a bully. There's no debating it!"

"Respectfully, sir, I must disagree with you. You have no idea what it's like to be a kid in today's world."

"True, I may not know exactly what it means to be a kid in today's world, but I do know a bully when I see one."

"How would you know?" I asked.

"I know because I used to be a bully," Mr. Phillips said.

"Huh? You used to be a bully?"

"Yep. I was a bully for most of my childhood."

"No way! I don't believe you." Adults were always making things up so they could relate to us. There was no way Mr. Phillips, the Random Acts of Kindness guru, used to be a bully. I didn't buy it!

"Unfortunately, it's true. I was a bully until my sophomore year of high school. In fact, you can ask Mrs. Grant. She was my English teacher in ninth and tenth grade. I still hold the record for most office referrals in one year at Forest Ridge High School."

"So, you're saying you're famous?"

"No, far from it! I'm not proud that I was

a bully. My actions hurt many people, and I spent numerous months apologizing to many of them. I hurt some people so deeply that it has taken years for them to get over the pain. The damage bullying causes isn't always visible, and that's the sad part. When we bully others, we stand the chance of ruining the lives of innocent people. I had to learn the hard way, but I am grateful that I had teachers that cared enough to stand by me as I learned to do better."

"Why are you telling me this?"

"I'm telling you this so you can find the courage to make positive changes. You see this folder on my desk?"

"Yeah, what about it?"

"It's your school records. I looked them over before coming to get the three of you. Up until the end of fourth grade, your teachers had wonderful things to say about you." Mr. Phillips pulled out a sticky note tucked inside my folder. "Here are just a few of the wonderful things your former teachers had to say about you. First grade, 'Tyler loves learning and is a great friend to his classmates.' Second grade, 'Tyler is a hard worker and a wonderful role model for others.' Third grade, 'Tyler enjoys learning and collaborating with others. He is the perfect gentleman.' So, Tyler, tell me, what changed?"

"Nothing . . . I mean, I don't know." I could feel my face turn red from discomfort. A sick feeling hit my stomach.

"Okay, I'm not going to force you to tell me. Mrs. Russell and I are here for you when you are ready. For now, you and your friends will have to face the consequences of your actions."

"Out-of-school suspension?"

"No, you will serve in-school suspension and will spend some time with Mrs. Russell reviewing our school's RAK Initiative.

"I already know about the RAK stuff," I blurted without thinking.

"Well, then you will have no problem thinking of some acts of kindness that will counteract your negative actions this morning," Mr. Phillips said as he handed me a referral slip.

"I can hardly wait."

I didn't plan for my response to be coated in sarcasm; it just came out that way. Mr. Phillips did not react. He stood quietly for several seconds, and then directed me toward the office waiting area where Cameron and Miguel were sitting quietly.

"Tyler, please sit in the seat by the door, and wait for Mrs. Russell to come get you. As for all three of you, I expect you to act responsibly, and that's not a suggestion."

The three of us nodded our heads, and we sat and waited. Unfortunately, the short wait became a long wait, and I grew restless. This day needed to be over.

REFLECTIONS

I TOSSED AND TURNED in my bed for the hundredth time. It was Saturday morning, and the apartment was quiet. Since I couldn't sleep, I stared at the ceiling. Reflections of yesterday's events circled through my thoughts. I could hear Mr. Phillip's words replay in my mind. *"I was a bully for most of my childhood, and I'm not proud of it. The damage bullying causes isn't always visible, and that's the sad part."* Could he be telling the truth? For some reason, I believe he was being honest, and that's what makes it even scarier. He shared a personal story, and that's not something most administrators do.

I thought I'd been practicing self-preservation, but maybe I was wrong. I know there's been a change in me since Dad left, but I thought the change had made me stronger. Now I act to try to stop the hurt before it comes, but it still keeps coming. Have I become a bully? No, it can't be possible. I've always been the good kid, the one that teachers compliment . . . well, used to compliment.

Adults just don't get it. Life is easier for them. Okay, I need to stop thinking about this for now. It's all too confusing. Besides, Dad will be here in a few hours to pick me up. We're going to the camping store to buy supplies for my birthday trip. Yep, I'm going to think about my birthday trip with Dad. That will make me feel better for sure. This trip will make up for the one we didn't get to take this past summer. It will happen this time, and I'll have some exciting details to share with my classmates.

My stomach rumbled, so I got out of bed and headed to the kitchen to find something good to eat. Mom had gone shopping last night, so I had the choice of three different kinds of cereal and two kinds of Pop-Tarts. I settled on Honey Nut Cheerios and a strawberry Pop-Tart. It didn't take me long to shovel down my breakfast, and my choices hit the spot. I rushed back to my room and picked out my clothes for the day. If I took a quick shower and didn't waste any time getting dressed, I'd have some time to play a few video games before Dad got here. Oh, wait, Mom took video game privileges away yesterday. No problem, I'll read my comic books.

As I got out of the shower, I heard the phone ring. After a few minutes, Mom called out from the kitchen.

"Tyler!"

"Yeah, I'm getting dressed," I shouted from my bedroom door.

"Please hurry. Your dad is on the phone and needs to speak with you."

"Tell him we can talk when he gets here."

"He says he needs to speak with you now."

"Okay, give me one minute to finish dressing." Why does Dad need to speak with me now? He should be getting ready to come pick me up. Maybe he wants to take me to breakfast. That makes sense. Even though I have already eaten, I could still go for some pancakes or French toast. I put on my jeans and shirt and ran to the kitchen.

"I'm here, Mom."

She handed me the phone, and I sat at the counter.

"Hey, Dad! Even though I had some cereal earlier, I'm good with getting breakfast first!" I took my chances and cut to the chase, so I could finish getting ready.

"Hey, son! Although breakfast sounds good, it will have to wait."

"Oh, I thought that's why you were calling. Sorry, Dad. So, what's up? Are you already on your way?"

"No, I'm still home. Ty, your mom and I have been talking about your recent behavior at school, and I think we should postpone our shopping trip until next week."

"Huh? No, Dad! I didn't do anything wrong yesterday. No one was hurt. Please don't cancel for today. I'm almost ready. We can discuss it during the drive. It's not even that bad. Come on, Dad! Please!"

"No, Tyler. There are always consequences for inappropriate behavior. I need you to understand that your actions are not acceptable. Waiting will give you time to correct your actions. Besides, we still have plenty of time to get the necessary supplies before the trip."

"But, Dad, it was all a misunderstanding!"

"Ty, you're not going to change my mind. I suggest you complete any missing work and do your chores. I've got to go now. We'll talk later in the week."

"You promise?"

"Yes, I promise."

"Okay, but—"

"We can talk about it when I see you next time. Until then, make better choices, Ty.

"Okay, Dad." I paused and tried to compose myself before continuing, "I love you."

I didn't hear a response back, so I tried again. "Dad, I ..." and realized that Dad had already hung up.

A mix of emotions welled up in me, but I did everything I could to keep them in check. My outing with Dad was supposed to make this lousy week better, but now I'll have to settle for plain lousy. If that loser had not shown up, Friday would have never happened. It's all his fault, and there will be paybacks. Yep, paybacks are coming, R.J., and your friends won't be able to help you. Just hope we don't come face to face anytime soon.

CHAPTER 25

THE DIFFERENCE OF A WEEK

THE WEEK FOLLOWING THE in-school suspension was pretty low-key, but my anger was still stewing. I did my best to keep it in check and avoid the students in Mr. Bailey's class, especially R.J. Our class focused on being strategic during kickball practices. We are pretty good, and I know Mr. Bailey's class doesn't have a chance of winning the tournament, especially with that loser. The trophy is ours this year, Mr. Bailey! You might as well start crying over your loss now, so you don't embarrass yourself after the tournament.

Thankfully, Dad also kept his promise,

and we spent Saturday morning at Next Adventure, one of the best outdoor sporting shops in Portland. Dad even made time in our schedule to grab lunch at the Pine Street Market.

"Ty, how did your week go?" Dad asked as he took a large bite of his burger.

"Pretty low-key for the most part. My grades are good, and our class is killing it during kickball practices. Mrs. Granger made me one of the pitchers. She said my quick response and intimidating looks make me the perfect choice."

"Intimidating looks?" Dad said, now looking concerned.

"Yeah. I have this look I give before I pitch the ball. It makes the kicker nervous."

"Interesting. So, let me see this look."

"I can't do it on demand."

"I'm sure you can. Come on, give it to me!"

"Okay, I'll try."

Dad was staring at me. Tightening my jaw and squinting my eyes, I gave it my best shot. His eyebrows rose in surprise as he pulled his head back, but his look broke my focus, and we both started laughing.

***

Dad and I had a good time together on our outing, which put me in a pretty good mood. I spent the rest of the weekend hanging out with Cameron and Miguel. We played video games and made some time to ride our bikes.

Overall, the last seven days have been great and I hope it stays that way. I didn't get into any trouble at school, and I managed to avoid the losers in Mr. Bailey's class. Maybe some time away from them will help me calm down. After all, my birthday trip planning is coming along well, and this time, it will happen.

CLOSE ENCOUNTERS OF OPPOSITE KINDS

I'M NOT USUALLY A big fan of Monday mornings, but the weekend events and the fact that my birthday is almost here made it easier for me to press through the start of another mundane week. It wasn't helping that the weather forecast for the week was bleak. We're supposed to have lots of rain for the next four days. The rain will affect recess and kickball practice, but it will not get in the way of my birthday camping trip! Dad and I purchased all the right gear to handle downpours, mud, and any lingering puddles. We're good to go no matter the weather! Fortunately, the weekend weather looks promising, especially in Gresham, where Oxbow Regional Park is located.

The bus ride to school was quiet because Miguel and Cameron weren't riding today. Cameron's mother drove him to school because she had to be at work earlier than usual, and Miguel would be late because he had a dental appointment. As I walked toward my classroom, I realized that I had left my backpack on the bus. I turned around and rushed toward the stairwell. Suddenly, I was face-to-face with R.J. He looked at me dumbfounded and then, after a short pause, said, "Hey, Ty!"

Hey, Ty? Are you kidding me? How does this loser think he can greet me as if we are friends? What is he thinking? The feelings I had managed to keep in check began surfacing, and something overcame me. I grabbed his lunch bag intending to crush its contents, but instead, I tossed it into the trash can. I mumbled "loser" under my breath and kept walking. The hall was empty, so, fortunately, there were no witnesses. I'm pretty sure R.J. is too much of a wimp to tell anyone what I did, so I shook it off and kept going.

As I got closer to the bus entrance, a little

girl tripped and fell right in front of me. She started whimpering, and that stopped me dead in my tracks. I helped her up and noticed her laces were untied. That was likely the cause of her fall. I offered to tie her laces, and an instant smile appeared on her tear-stained face.

"What's your name?"

"Tyler," I said.

"Tyler, I like that name. My name is Natalia."

"Natalia . . . that's a cool name. I need to hurry and get my backpack off the bus before my driver leaves."

"Okay, and I need to get to my class," she said.

I continued on my mission, but before I made it out the door, I felt a tug on the back of my jacket. I turned to see Natalia, and before I knew it, she hugged me and said, "Tyler, you are the kindest big kid in this school. Thank you for helping me!"

Her words paralyzed me, and feelings of guilt washed over me. How can I be the kindest big kid in the whole school after what I did upstairs? I don't like these mixed feelings that have overcome me, but I maintained my composure. After giving me another big smile,

Natalia skipped away, and I ran toward the bus. My attitude and emotions were having a game of tug of war, and I was not sure which was winning. I wanted to go home, but that was not an option. So far, it hasn't been a great start to the week, and I hope it's not a sign of things to come.

CHAPTER 27

HOW DID IT ALL GO WRONG?

FRIDAY IS FINALLY HERE, and the excitement of the upcoming camping trip proved more distracting than I anticipated. Camping at Oxbow is not as epic as the white water rapids trip was going to be, but with fishing, hiking, and late-night stargazing, we have all the makings of a phenomenal birthday weekend. Plus, getting to spend quality time with Dad, which had rarely happened since the split, was a big thing. Although I left several messages for Dad on Thursday evening, I still hadn't heard back from him as of this morning. I'm sure he worked late last night to have a work-free weekend. Yep, that's the most likely explanation. No distractions means I will get Dad all to myself.

When I entered my classroom, I heard students whispering about the strange substitute in Mr. Bailey's class. Apparently, she is not like most substitutes that frequent Fern Creek Elementary. She has long pink hair, dresses in some retro-like fashion, and speaks with a British accent. I'm curious to get a peek at her, but the late bell rings, and Mrs. Granger is front and center, ready to begin our morning meeting.

"Good morning, class! The rain appears to have moved on, and we can expect some sunshine today. The field is riddled with puddles, so kickball practice doesn't seem promising for the fifth consecutive day. However, next week's forecast looks great. Now let's begin our day. This morning's kindness quote was first spoken by Albert Schweitzer, a recipient of the Nobel Peace Prize in 1952."

Cameron interrupted, "Were you a teacher in 1952?"

"Cameron Parks, are you serious? Do I look that old?" asked Mrs. Granger.

"Uh, no. I guess not. Sorry." Cameron's face turned red as everyone stared at him in disbelief.

"For your information, I've been teaching for almost twenty-five years, so, no, I wasn't teaching in 1952. In fact, I wasn't born until almost two decades later," Mrs. Granger said, giving a wink, before continuing. "Now back to the quote. 'Constant kindness can accomplish much. As the sun makes ice melt, kindness causes misunderstanding, mistrust, and hostility to evaporate.'" Mrs. Granger repeated the quote before she paused and waited for students to comment or ask questions.

Hands began to pop up. Mrs. Granger scanned the room and smiled when she spotted Ava's raised hand. "Ava, thank you for participating. What are your comments or questions?"

"In science, we studied the effects of the sun on the water cycle. Thanks to you, we all know that evaporation happens when the sun heats the water left behind in puddles into water vapor. The water is no longer visible, and the nasty puddles that get mud all over your new boots dry up. I guess kindness is like the sun. The more kindness happens, the quicker it evaporates the bad stuff that makes people grumpy. I kind of get grumpy when there are muddy puddles everywhere. The mud messes up my new boots, which take forever to clean.

Wait, sorry, Mrs. Granger, I've lost my train of thought."

"No worries, Ava. I also hate how muddy puddles mess up my shoes, and I believe the first part of your comment is perfect."

"Thanks, Mrs. Granger," said Ava, now sporting red blotches on her neck from embarrassment.

The phone on Mrs. Granger's desk rang, and the conversation paused while she answered it.

"Hello, this is Mrs. Granger. Yes, he's here. Oh . . . I see. Hmm, that's disappointing. Sure, I will let him know. Thanks. Bye." By this point, every student is wondering which boy will get some news that doesn't sound too promising. Mrs. Granger took a few seconds to process the conversation before looking up. A forced smile appeared on her face as she pointed to me and said, "Mr. Miller, may I have a quick word with you outside the classroom?"

"Yes, Mrs. Granger," I answered, hoping the news was related to the awful traffic that paralyzed Portland's roads every Friday. Dad probably wanted to pick me up early from school so we could get ahead of the rush hour traffic. Of course, this news would disappoint Mrs. Granger because I will miss the math test. I walked outside the classroom behind Mrs. Granger. She was biting her lower lip, and I concluded that the news had nothing to do with traffic.

"I'm sorry, but I have some disappointing news for you, Tyler. Your dad called the office about ten minutes ago and left a message for you. Unfortunately, he has an emergency at work and has to cancel your weekend camping trip plans. I'm sorry, Tyler."

My body instantly felt limp, and I could feel tears welling up in the corners of my eyes. I was stunned but managed to produce a nervous smile. I felt a sudden urge to run. Instead, I took a deep breath and asked Mrs. Granger if I could use the restroom before returning to class.

"Sure, Tyler. Please do. Once again, I'm sorry to be the one to share this disappointing news with you."

"It's okay, Mrs. Granger," I said before walking quickly toward the gang bathroom.

Thankfully, the bathroom was empty. I entered the first stall and locked the door behind me. The tears I managed to hold back began pouring out uncontrollably. How could Dad do this to me again? Why is his job more important than me, his son? Is this my payback for what I did to that loser on Monday? The tears rolled down my cheeks, and my body was shaking. I was so angry and hurt. Then an unexpected voice caught me off guard. I held my breath.

"Are you okay? Should I call someone?"

"No. Just leave," I responded. There was something oddly familiar about this voice. After a brief silence, there was a faint knock on the stall door.

"I said leave!"

"No," he said. "Let me help you, please."

"You can't help me! Just get out!"

"Maybe if you tell me what's wrong, I could help you."

"Maybe if you tell me what's wrong, I could help you," I mocked. "Right!"

"Try me." His voice sounded shaky.

"It's nothing. My dad just bailed on me again," I said without pause.

"Are your parents . . ."

"Divorced! My dad was supposed to take me camping for my birthday this weekend. He promised that he would the last time he canceled!"

"This is your birthday weekend?" the voice asked.

"Yeah! It's already ruined," I said, hoping the conversation would stop.

"I get how you're feeling."

"Yeah? And how would you know?" I was wondering who had the nerve to meddle in my business.

"Well, I haven't seen my dad in a while," he answered.

"Are your parents divorced?" I asked, trying to piece the mystery together.

"No," he said.

"So, why haven't you seen your dad?" Curiosity got the best of me.

"It's complicated," he said.

"When is he coming home?" I probed, hoping that he would say something to make my situation seem not as bad.

"I'm not sure when, but I know he will."

"Yeah, well, good for you. How does that help me?" My tone was now more sarcastic than curious.

"I know it doesn't help you, but I get how you're feeling right now."

"Riiight, sure you do!" I snapped. Is this kid for real? What a total loser!

"No, really, I kinda do. It's hard, but you need to keep a positive outlook."

"Hey, who are you?" A sinking feeling hit me in the pit of my stomach. I've heard this voice recently.

"It's . . . R.J."

"What? Are you kidding me? Get out of here and leave me alone!"

"But I really need to pee!"

"Go downstairs to another bathroom!" I yelled, hoping he would finally leave me alone.

"I won't make it. Please, I really need to go!" he pleaded.

"Fine! You better not say anything!" This encounter is going to mess things up for me. He needs to mind his business if he knows what's good for him.

"About what?" he asked.

"Just do your business and get out!" This kid is either braver than I thought or the biggest loser ever! I heard him run to the farthest stall from mine. The stall door shut abruptly. I grabbed a wad of toilet tissue and wiped away the tears. I needed to leave before R.J. finished his business. Suddenly, I heard someone else enter the bathroom.

"Ty!" called Cameron.

"Yeah!" I answered while grabbing some fresh tissue.

"Mrs. Granger sent me to check on you. We're about to start the test. Are you coming?"

"What's her problem? Tell her I'll be there in a minute and get out!"

"Okay, okay! You're sure in a bad mood today!"

"Whatever! Just go!" As soon as Cameron left, I took a deep breath, opened the stall door, and made my way to the sink. I splashed some cold water on my splotchy face and grabbed a paper towel to dry off. R.J. walked to the sink beside me and began washing his hands. He did not talk to me—a wise choice. As I turned to leave, I heard him whisper, "I forgive you."

Huh? Did I hear right? He forgives me? Are you kidding me? I felt my emotions resurfacing, and without thinking, I clenched my left fist and began raising my arm. Realizing what I was about to do, I froze. My mind flooded with waves of questions. Was I actually going to hit him? Did R.J. deserve to be treated this way? Have I really and truly become a bully? I can't face these questions right now, so I took a deep breath, relaxed my arm, and kept walking, not once looking back at R.J. How did this day go so wrong?

I DIDN'T SEE THAT COMING

I MANAGED TO MAKE it through the morning, but I don't believe the math test score will reflect my actual ability. I couldn't focus no matter how hard I tried. Between Dad canceling the camping trip and my encounter with R.J., my emotions were on a roller coaster ride to an unknown destination. I don't recognize the person I have become, and now, I'm prime for a payback. I was shocked when R.J. reported me to Mr. Bailey for throwing his lunch in the trash. I didn't think he had the guts to do it. Now R.J. has enough ammunition to roast me with our classmates, and I can't blame him if he does. I've laughed at his expense since that unfortunate event on the kickball field. Yeah, I really am prime for payback.

The morning faded into the afternoon, and my body now felt numb from the battle raging inside me. Lunch was a blur, and recess, limited to the asphalt area thanks to all the rain, was uneventful until Ms. Simmons, the intriguing substitute covering for Mr. Bailey, walked over to me.

"Hello, young man!" she said, giving me a friendly smile. Her accent was definitely British, and she looked like a character from Alice in Wonderland. The Mad Hatter, to be exact.

"Hello," I said, unsure why she was talking to me.

"My name is Ms. Simmons, and I am subbing today for Mr. Bailey. I've been observing you since lunch."

"You have? Why? Did R.J. say something to you? Am I in trouble?" I could feel my cheeks flush.

"No and no. Relax for a moment. I can tell there is a battle brewing inside you."

"You can?" I said in surprise.

"Yes, I can. I faced an internal battle many years ago, so I am familiar with the outward look. Are you keen to hear a bit of advice?"

"Keen?"

"We Brits use that word as a synonym for eager or willing," she said.

"Oh, that makes sense now."

"So, are you keen?"

"Yes, sorry, ma'am!"

Ms. Simmons laughed, then said, "Ma'am—I've never been called ma'am before. It makes me feel older, like my mum."

"Mum?"

"Mom. Mum is how we Brits say it."

"Got it. So, what is your advice?" My curiosity had increased.

"It's a quote I penciled in my special notebook a while back. I'm a collector of quotes, especially those that speak purpose to my life."

I nodded my head as a polite acknowledgment. Ms. Simmons proceeded to open her bag and pull out a journal. She thumbed through its worn pages and began skimming the handwritten entries. "Ah, here it is. It's a quote by the late Robert Schuller. 'Let your hopes, not your hurts, shape your future,'" she read.

I was unsure how to respond, so I didn't say anything.

"Do you understand what it means, luv?" she asked.

"I think so."

"I'm sorry if I am overstepping, but I felt you needed to hear those words today and truly take them to heart. Let me repeat them, and then I'll leave you alone. 'Let your hopes, not your hurts, shape your future.'" A faint smile appeared on her face as she waited for my response.

"Thank you, Ms. Simmons."

"Cheers, my new friend. Keep that chin up. Your best days are coming." She gave me a wink, closed her journal, slipped it back into her bag, and headed back toward Mr. Bailey's class.

I didn't see that coming. How could Ms. Simmons see my inner turmoil? The quote replayed in my thoughts for the remainder of the day.

CHAPTER 29

SOMETIMES THE TRUTH IS HARD TO ADMIT

WHEN I ARRIVED HOME after a horrible day at school, surprisingly, Mom was already there. She was busy preparing dinner in the small kitchen, and, I must admit, it smelled incredible. Since I hadn't eaten lunch, my stomach began growling uncontrollably. Mom isn't typically home this early, especially on a Friday. And she definitely doesn't put this much effort in the kitchen during the week.

"What is going on?" I asked.

"Oh, not much," she said, adding a bowlful of vegetables to the sizzling wok.

"Not much? Mom, you're home early on a Friday and cooking up a storm. Something is going on."

"One of my favorite people of all time has a birthday this weekend, so I thought we should kick off the weekend with my famous sesame chicken with stir-fried veggies! What do you think, birthday boy?"

"I don't feel much like celebrating," I answered.

"I know you're upset about your dad canceling the camping trip, and rightfully so. But he truly has a work emergency."

"He does? What kind of emergency?"

"Your dad was contacted early this morning by his law firm's sister firm in Chicago. Apparently, the head prosecuting attorney needs your dad's military experience with surveillance to help them win a case. The Chicago firm has been working on a huge case that is being televised."

"Are you for real?"

"Yes. This is a huge break for your dad."

"Wow, I had no idea. I just thought Dad would rather work than spend time with me."

"Honey, that's not the case. Your dad was truly upset about canceling."

"How do you know?"

"We spoke this morning before he called the school. We also spoke at length while I drove him to the airport."

"You didn't go to work today?"

"I called out of work after speaking with your dad. He needed my help to get to the airport."

"Oh, that's good, I guess."

"Honey, I know you were looking forward to the camping trip. I get it. Dad promised to make it up to us after the trial ends."

"Make it up to us?" I was not sure why Mom included herself.

"Well, your dad and I thought we could go as a family."

"As a family?" I asked. This day was growing more confusing by the minute.

"Yes, as a family. Your dad and I are hoping to work things out."

"Wait! Did you say work things out?"

"Yes. We've been talking about it for a while. We plan to take it slowly, but I think it is promising."

I cannot believe what I'm hearing. Mom and Dad are working it out even though I overheard the dreaded divorce word . . . when did this happen? How did it happen? How did I miss it? At this point, I don't care about knowing the answers to all my questions. This is the best news I've heard all day. But as much as I wanted this news to wash over my disappointment and hurt, a heavy cloud still weighed over me.

"Honey, aren't you happy?"

"Yeah, it's just . . . ."

"I know Dad won't be here for your birthday."

"No, it's not that, Mom."

"Did something happen at school today?"

"Uhm, yeah, sort of . . . it's hard to explain," I said with some hesitation.

"I don't understand. Did I miss a message from Mrs. Granger or Mr. Phillips?" Mom picked up her cell phone and scanned through her messages and emails.

"No. Something almost happened, but it's more what I realized that is bothering me."

"Ty, what did you realize?"

"Uhm, it's kind of embarrassing to admit. I realized that I've become . . . sort of like . . . no, not sort of . . . I realized that I've become a bully." I finally said the word out loud.

"Honey, if you recall our conversation in

January, I told you that your actions were those of a bully. It was not easy saying that to you."

"Yeah, I remember that conversation. It made me upset. I thought you were wrong, so I dismissed your words. But then, this morning, I saw it for myself. Mom, somehow I have become a bully without realizing it. It's not who I used to be, but sadly, it's who I am now."

"No, that's not true, Ty! You can change this reality. You can do it. Ask Mr. Phillips. I'm sure he can help you. Or you could start participating in the RAK Initiative."

"It's too late."

"Honey, it's never too late to become a better person. It takes work, but with each effort, it gets easier. I promise."

"But what about all the people I've already hurt?"

"In time, you will find a way to mend those fences."

"What if I can't do it?"

"Ty, the fact that you're admitting you've become a bully makes me know that you can do it." Mom put out her arms to hug me, and after a moment I felt more confident.

This day has been a whirlwind of emotions and not at all what I had expected when

I left the apartment this morning. I'm unsure how I will navigate the next few days, let alone the last few weeks of school. How will I react if R.J. retaliates? I've given him the perfect setup for revenge, and right before the kickball tournament, no less. It will be hard to take, but I'll have to endure it if there's any hope for a positive change.

CHAPTER 30

THE KICKBALL TOURNAMENT

IT'S WEDNESDAY AT LAST. The weather is perfect with no chance of rain in the forecast. My class was able to practice on Tuesday, and from what I can tell, we have a great chance of winning the kickball tournament. Unfortunately, Mr. Bailey will need counseling because his class will not win this year. That's not a putdown; it's the truth based on weeks of observation.

Since I held it together this past week, Mrs. Granger asked me to serve as a pitcher in the tournament before I left school yesterday. Her news made me smile even though I still couldn't think of a way to repair the damage I had done to R.J. He didn't take advantage of my weakest moment. If it had been the other way around and I had walked in on R.J. crying, I would have used it against him. I expected retaliation from him and his friends on Monday or yesterday, but nothing. When he whispered, "I forgive you," I thought he was kidding. Now, I see that he meant every word. It wasn't an empty promise like those I've experienced these past months. Today will be brutal for him. Not to be mean, but he really can't play kickball. The odds are not in his favor, but I hope he doesn't pass out again. That would not be good, especially since all the fourth grade classes will be watching.

We were one of the first classes out on the field. Mrs. Granger likes to be early, and from what I can tell, she is exceptionally pumped for today's tournament. Within minutes, the other fifth grade classes began arriving on the field. The fourth grade classes followed and found their spots on the sidelines. Mrs. Grant was front and center and smiled as she scanned the field. From what I've heard, this is a big deal for the staff and students of Fern Creek Elementary. Mrs. Grant made her way to the microphone and began speaking.

"Good morning, fifth grade competitors and fourth grade onlookers! We are so excited to announce the start of our Annual Fifth Grade Kickball Tournament. Before we begin, we will recite the Pledge of Allegiance."

With one voice, we recited the pledge, and it sounded like we were at a professional sporting event.

Mrs. Grant continued, "Now, let's all recite our school pledge."

"As students of Fern Creek Elementary, we pledge to show kindness in all our words and actions in the hope that we will make a true difference in our school and the world beyond!"

For the first time, the overarching theme of the kindness pledge struck a chord in me. Our actions can positively impact the world around us. Unfortunately, my actions have been far more negative than positive over the last few months. I'm not proud of this, but I hope to change before I'm too far gone. I want my future impact to be positive, if possible. The world can be harsh, but we can choose to be kind. I know this now. I'm going to try my best. It may not be enough, but it's a start. As the students began cheering, my attention returned to the tournament.

"Let's play kickball!" shouted Mrs. Grant, raising her hands toward the sky. She was pretty enthusiastic about this tournament, more than I imagined. Suddenly, the crowd roared with excitement as the fifth grade teachers came running onto the field wearing cheerleader uniforms. They looked utterly ridiculous, and I wanted to turn to Cameron and Miguel and make a snarky comment, but I quickly realized that my initial response was wrong. As I came to my senses, Mr. Bailey did an impressive back flip, and the teachers started performing a dance routine while "Eye of the Tiger" played in the background. Oddly, that's my dad's favorite song. Again, my first instinct was to make a snide remark, but I decided to enjoy the moment. They were actually pretty impressive. As the music finished, our class made its way to the dugout. We were up first against Mr. Bailey's class. James, who is all about sports, was up to kick first.

"Go, Ja-mers!" our class shouted. His face grew even more serious. Thomas, one of the best players in Mr. Bailey's class, was the pitcher. He sent the ball barreling toward James, and the ball went flying through the air toward third base. Unfortunately, some kid caught it, and James was out.

"You're out!" bellowed Mr. Phillips, the official umpire for today's tournament.

Cameron was up next. He made a base hit. Laynie and Lexi also made base hits, and now the bases were loaded. I'm next. This will be an easy four runs. Thomas pitched and I ran toward the ball. As my foot hit the ball, I realized that it would be a foul. No problem. The next kick will be the winner. As the ball rolled my way, I began running and then kicked. There was a loud crack when my foot impacted the ball. It went flying toward Jennilee, and I started running. Surprisingly, she caught the ball after one bounce, tagged Laynie as she approached second base, and then threw the ball toward home plate. Thomas caught the ball without fail and tagged Cameron before his foot touched home plate.

"Three outs! Switch!" shouted Mr. Phillips. Wow, I didn't expect Mr. Bailey's class to be that good on the field. They were showing out today. We switched places, and it was my turn to pitch.

On my first pitch, Zoe kicked a foul. On my second pitch, Zoe kicked it and made it safely to second base. Andy was up next for Mr. Bailey's class. He is the one that reported me to Mr. Phillips, but I needed to let it go. I pitched the ball, and Andy hit it straight over the second baseman's head. He made it safely to second base, but Zoe stopped at third. Good choice. The quiet girl, Ella, was up. I pitched the ball, and it was gone. She kicked a homer, and I was in shock. Mr. Bailey's class was winning by three points. I underestimated Mr. Bailey's class. Thomas, their pitcher, was up next. I pitched, and he kicked a fly ball, which I caught easily. One out! Sophie was next, and she made it to first base. Blake followed, and since our second baseman missed the ball, Sophie made it safely to second base as Blake arrived on first. Still only one out. I needed to improve my game. Jennilee was up next. I've got this one. Her first three attempts were all fouls. My game was improving. Jennilee kicked it on the fourth pitch, and it flew directly into my arms! Two out and one more to go! Another kid, whose name I don't know, kicked the ball down the first baseline. He was super fast and made it to base before Cameron tagged him.

"You're safe!" shouted Mr. Phillips.

The bases were now loaded, and I was not happy. It was time to increase the speed of my pitches. A girl started walking toward home plate but suddenly did a one-eighty and made her way to Mr. Bailey. After a few seconds, I heard Mr. Phillips call a time-out. Mr. Bailey and the girl were talking. I saw him motion for the nurse. The nurse helped the girl sit down, then handed her some juice. Mr. Bailey picked up the megaphone and said, "Emma's going to be fine. She just needs to sit out for a while. Move on to the next player."

"Let's go, R.J.! You're up!" Thomas shouted.

"You can do it, R.J.!" Blake cheered from second base.

"Remember, feel the rhythm!" Ella added from the fence.

I'm sorry to say this, but this will be our third out. R.J.'s not good at sports, and no matter how much his classmates cheer him on, he will fail. I feel bad because I know he tried to help me last Friday, and although he had every right to seek revenge, he didn't. His choices have been better than mine, so I must find a way to make it right between us before the school year ends. For now, no matter what R.J. does in the next few minutes, I won't laugh or make fun of him.

R.J. walked to home plate. He looked nervous, which made me anxious for him. I felt my emotions rising, but I needed to keep focused. As I stared straight ahead and got ready to pitch the ball, I prepared for the worst. I watched as R.J. took several steps back, waiting for me to launch the ball. I released the ball, and it headed straight for him. R.J. started running, closed his eyes, and kicked the ball. His foot hit the ball straight on, creating a loud crack. As the ball soared through the air, everyone started cheering, especially Mr. Bailey's class.

"Run, R.J.! Run!" Mr. Bailey's class shouted.

I watched in surprise as he made it to first base. The crowd was chanting, "Run! Run! Run!" As he touched second base, the crowd kept cheering and R.J. continued to run. He made it to home plate before the ball came back to me. I was in complete awe. When did he learn to kick the ball like that? Without thinking, I stretched out my arm, raised my thumb, and yelled out, "Way to go, R.J! That was AWE-some!" I know he heard me because he immediately looked my way. His expression was frozen, but seconds later, his classmates whisked him into a frenzy of high fives and cheers, and I wondered if he accepted my compliment. Then it hit me. I was willingly being kind for the first time in a long time. Maybe Mom was right and I really could change for the better.

Mr. Bailey's class won that game. And oddly enough, I believe I won too because I've taken steps toward a better path no matter the outcome. Standing on the sidelines as the other classes played, I recalled the quote outside Mrs. Granger's door, "Courage is fire, and bullying is smoke." The first time I saw this quote, I dismissed it as nonsense because it didn't mean anything to me. Today, I finally realized how much truth was packed into those seven words.

A CONVERSATION WITH MOM

"DID YOUR CLASS WIN the kickball tournament?" Mom asked as she entered the apartment carrying a bag of groceries.

"Surprisingly, no."

"Really? So, who won?" she asked as she began emptying the bags.

"Mr. Bailey's class. They will hold the title for another year."

"Interesting. I thought you said they didn't have a chance this year."

"They didn't, but somehow R.J., a new kid, learned how to kick the ball. His improvement was impressive."

"Well, good for him. I guess you should never underestimate the underdog."

"You're right, Mom. I thought losing would feel more disappointing, but it doesn't. I am happy for R.J. and for Mr. Bailey's class."

"Tyler Eric Miller, I believe you are changing for the better!"

With Mom's compliment, I could feel my neck and face turn red. I know she is right, but what if I can't keep moving in the right direction? Life is full of surprises and unexpected challenges that try to steer you off track.

"Mom?"

"Yes, honey."

"What if I revisit the wrong path?"

"Each day is an opportunity for growth, but growth can go both positive and negative. You must be mindful of every choice, and although not every decision will prove to be right, your intent must come from the right place," Mom said.

"I'm not sure I understand. How do I know if my intent comes from the right place?"

"Let kindness be the barometer for your intent," Mom said.

"Barometer, like in weather?"

"Not exactly. A weather barometer measures air pressure. In this case, the barometer measures the direction of your actions, whether positive or negative. Kindness always points us in a positive direction."

"Hmm, I get it now. I guess I should have been listening more to all the kindness quotes Mrs. Granger has shared since I came to Fern Creek."

"That might be true, but it's never too late to join the kindness journey. In fact, I'm sure I can pull up hundreds of kindness quotes in one Google search."

"I guess I've got some catching up to do. Thanks, Mom! Have you heard from Dad?"

"Yes. In fact, turn on the news, and we may see him."

"Huh?"

"Remember the case I told you about on Friday?"

"Yes. Oh, wait, you mentioned something about the case being televised."

"Glad you were listening. Yes, this case is a big deal and should be on all the major networks."

"So, why will Dad be on TV?"

"The Chicago lawyers was so impressed with your dad's skills, they decided to bring him on the case."

"Really? Wow, wait until Cameron and Miguel hear about this! My dad is famous."

"I don't know about famous, but it's a pretty big deal," Mom said.

It took me several minutes to find the TV remote, but the first channel I selected was a winner. As the cameras panned across the courtroom, there was Dad sitting next to a slightly older man.

"Look! There's Dad! He looks so serious."

"He's definitely got the serious look going on, but he's still the hottest guy in the room!" Mom added.

"T-M-I, Mom!" I exclaimed. It's always weird to hear your parents say stuff like this, but now I know that they really are working on their relationship. For the first time in a long while, life is looking up, which is better than any gift money can buy.

THERE ARE NO COINCIDENCES

THE WEEKS THAT FOLLOWED the kickball tournament and Dad's TV debut were pretty low-key, at least at school. We prepped for the end of the year assessments, and all the fifth grade classes began Sixth Grade Bootcamp. Mrs. Granger kicked off Bootcamp with a rap she wrote last year. Surprisingly, her performance, which included a few intriguing dance moves, was pretty solid. The class and I applauded when she finished. I still met with Mrs. Russell several times a week as recommended by Mr. Phillips. Mrs. Russell noticed a difference in my countenance—her words, not mine—and surprisingly, I shared the cause of the change. She listened intently as I shared the details, and, at one point, I noticed tears pooling in the corners of her eyes. She was proud of my efforts and encouraged me to stay on this positive path. Since we were completing our end-of-year assessments today, my visit with Mrs. Russell was rescheduled for the afternoon.

Sitting in Mrs. Russell's office after lunch, I listened intently to her words. With every word, I grew more confident that I was becoming the person I used to be—only better.

"Did you hear the news?" Mrs. Russell asked.

"Are you talking about my dad?"

"Your dad?"

"Yeah, my dad has been on the news for the last few weeks, and he and the persecuting attorney, I think that's what they call him—"

"I think you mean prosecuting attorney," she corrected.

"Yeah, that's it! Well, they won the case!"

"Wow, what a small world. Did you know that the dad of one of our students was a key witness in that case?"

"Really? Who?"

"You don't know?"

"No. Who is it? Is it someone in my class?"

"No, he's in Mr. Bailey's class. It's R.J."

"R.J.? Are you serious? I had no idea!"

"And there's a twist. His real name is Preston."

"His real name? I'm not following you."

"He and his family were in the witness protection program. They had to change their identities and appearances and move from Chicago to a new life in Portland overnight, without telling a single soul, including their extended family. And Preston is a bona fide music prodigy."

"A bona fide music prodigy? What does that mean?"

"A bona fide music prodigy is someone who is naturally gifted in the playing of an instrument. In R.J.'s case, he is a gifted cellist!"

"So Preston is a gifted cellist?"

"Yes."

"What's a cellist?"

"It's someone who plays the cello—"

"—the oversized violin. Yeah, I remember Mrs. Wells played the cello for us a few months ago when we were studying stringed instruments in music class. Wow, so he's really that good?"

"Yes, a real virtuoso."

"Mrs. Russell, are you trying to sneak in a vocabulary lesson? I'm guessing virtuoso means he's an above average player.

"Spot on, Tyler."

"So, what does R.J., I mean, Preston's dad look like?"

"He was the tall, blond gentleman the FBI used as a key witness."

"You mean the guy who wore the wire? That's Preston's dad?"

"Yes, that's him," said Mrs. Russell.

"Wow, that's crazy! My dad worked closely with him and reviewed all the evidence that was recorded over the wire."

"There are no coincidences, Tyler. Yet another reason why we should be kind to everyone we meet. We never know how paths may connect in the future."

"I had no idea that Preston's family was involved with this huge case. I'm sure he was worried about his dad." I thought about the conversation I had with Preston in the bathroom on one of my worst days. Now I understood why Preston said he knew how I was feeling. His life changed without his permission. Everything that happened was ultimately out of his control, and his dad could not be with him. In so many ways, that's what happened to me. I had been quick to dismiss what he said that day. If Preston hadn't said that he forgave me as I was leaving the restroom, I might not have realized how far from center my path had strayed. I could see now that Preston's actions were driven by kindness. I hope that I can repay his kindness before he goes back to his real life.

YEAH, IT'S NOT SELF-PRESERVATION

"WHAT'S GOTTEN INTO YOU?" Miguel asked me as the three of us walked toward the climbing wall during recess.

"What do you mean?" I asked, trying to pretend like I was oblivious to the direction of this conversation.

"Cameron, explain," Miguel said, giving him a nudge.

"Uh . . . It's like you've become, well, like a different person," Cameron said, returning Miguel's nudge.

"Yeah, I mean, you haven't made fun of

or picked on anyone in weeks," Miguel added.

"Why are you two acting so weird?" I asked.

"We're acting weird? Are you serious?" asked Cameron.

"Yeah, I am."

"Do you hear him?" Cameron asked, looking at Miguel.

"Calm down, guys! You're right. I've made some changes."

"Some changes? That's an understatement!" Miguel interjected.

"Dude, you're so dramatic," I said, trying not to laugh. "Okay, sorry. I couldn't resist. Before I explain, let me ask you one question. Do we still have fun hanging out together?"

"Yeah, of course. It's always fun when we're together," answered Miguel.

"Yeah, I agree," added Cameron.

"Okay, so we can agree that my changes haven't stopped us from having fun?"

"Yeah!" they answered.

"Well, then what's the problem?" I asked.

"You're exhausting, dude!" shouted Cameron.

"I'm just messing with you. A few weeks ago I realized that I had become someone I didn't like. As much as I hate to admit it, I had become a bully. In fact, we were all bullies."

"What? No way! We were just practicing self-preservation like you taught us."

"Cameron, that was a lie I told myself and tried to pass off as a justification for my actions—our actions."

"But it made sense."

"Yeah, Miguel, it's funny how we can justify our bad actions when it suits us."

"So, what made you change? Wait, did it have something to do with the day you were upset in the bathroom?" Cameron asked.

"Uhm, why do you ask?" I was curious how Cameron knew.

"Do you remember that Mrs. Granger sent me to check in on you? Somebody else was in there, and I'm pretty sure it was R.J.," Cameron said.

"And how would you know that?"

"I recognized his shoes—the ones he wore when he fainted on the field. You never told us exactly what happened in there," Cameron said looking at Miguel for support.

"Yeah, you're right. It was him. He overheard me crying after my dad had to cancel our camping trip again. Instead of minding his business, he tried to make me feel better. I wanted to hit R.J., I mean Preston, even though he didn't deserve it. He tried to help, but I nearly lost it when he said he forgave me!"

"Woah, he said that?"

"Yep, after everything I did to make his life miserable, he said, 'I forgive you.' Who does that? When I clenched my fist and began raising my arm, it hit me. I had crossed the line. Ironically, that kid has more talent than all of us combined. Who knew? And then, my dad and his dad worked together to take down some criminals."

"Yeah, that was crazy! Can you imagine having to change your identity and leave everyone you know and love?" added Miguel.

"No, I can't, and that's why I hate that I treated R.J., I mean Preston, so badly. He was going through a dark time, and so was I. We think we know people, but we don't. Everyone has a backstory, so that's why we should treat everyone kindly. Remember that unusual lady subbing for Mr. Bailey's class the day it all went down for me?"

"Yeah, how can anyone forget her? I mean, she stood out big time. Pink hair. Unusual clothing choices," said Miguel.

"All true, but despite her appearance, she was very perceptive."

"What do you mean?"

"She said something that has stuck with me since that day. It was a quote that she had scribbled in her journal. I can't remember who said it, but the message is powerful. 'Let your hopes, not your hurts, shape your future.' Guys, I became a bully because I allowed hurts to dictate my actions."

"That's deep. I knew that substitute was cool!" Cameron said.

"Has it been easy to make the change?" Miguel asked.

"Truth? No, it's been hard, but it gets a little easier with each day. I've had to catch myself a few times, well, maybe more than a few. I got so used to being sarcastic and laughing at people's expense. In time, I won't have to try so hard. At least, I hope so!"

"We can help!" interjected Cameron.

"Yeah, what he said!" agreed Miguel.

"Thanks, guys! We can do it together."

We heard Mrs. Granger's whistle blow in the distance and made our way back to line up. Recess was over for today, and after tomorrow, we would officially be middle schoolers. When

I started kindergarten, it seemed like a lifetime before this day would come. Today it feels like it came so quickly. So much has happened this year, and our lives have only just begun.

CHAPTER 34

THE LAST DAY OF FIFTH GRADE

IT'S THE LAST DAY of fifth grade at Fern Creek Elementary. All the student artwork, writings, and projects that covered the halls and classrooms were gone and the walls were bare. As I walked toward my classroom, I could feel different emotions floating through the warm air. While the start of summer was exciting, leaving your teacher and school would be sad for many fifth grade students. Although I had spent most of my elementary days at Woodland Park Elementary, the last five months at Fern Creek improved my life, so my time here has been important.

"Good morning, Tyler!" Mrs. Granger said as I walked into the room.

"Good morning, Mrs. Granger."

"Mr. Phillips would like to see you first thing this morning. If you don't mind, please make your way to the office before we begin our day."

"Sure. But did I do something wrong?"

"No. I don't believe so. No, I'm sure it has nothing to do with behavior. Besides, your attitude and behavior have been impeccable for the past month. It's as if you've become the best version of yourself—a perfect gentleman."

"Aww, thanks, Mrs. Granger! I'm glad you've noticed."

"Honestly, Tyler, I am so proud of you and the turnaround you have made. The potential was always there. I saw it the morning you walked into this classroom with your mom and Mr. Phillips. It was up to you to walk in your truth."

"I'm glad Mr. Phillips placed me in your classroom that day." I felt my neck and face begin to turn red. It had been a long time since I had received a compliment from anyone.

"Me too! You better make your way to the office before I start crying. It's not a pretty sight, and besides, I need my makeup to last until the end of the day."

"Yes, ma'am," I said and headed down the hall at a pretty good pace.

I slowed down as I got closer to the office. I had no idea why Mr. Phillips needed to see me on the last day. Maybe he wanted to compliment the changes I have made in my behavior. I don't believe I've done anything wrong since my last visit to the office, but I'm not one hundred percent certain. I hear some voices coming my way. It's Mrs. Grant and Ella. They were excited about something. I could hear part of their conversation as we crossed paths.

"When we get there, give me about thirty seconds to talk with Mr. Bailey before you share the news. The announcement will go out to every family in about thirty minutes," said Mrs. Grant.

"Thank you, Mrs. Grant. I can't wait until Preston hears the news," Ella said as the two continued toward the fifth grade hall.

News? Something is definitely going on. I sure hope I haven't done anything wrong. Well, here goes nothing. I walked into the front office.

"Hey, Tyler! Mr. Phillips is expecting you. Just take a seat. He'll be with you in a few minutes," the receptionist said.

"Okay. Thanks, Mrs. Clifton," I said, trying to sport a smile.

Five minutes, a mere three-hundred seconds, seemed like an eternity today as I waited for Mr. Phillips to come out of his office.

"Hey, Tyler! Thanks for waiting," Mr. Phillips said, standing in his office doorway.

"No problem, Mr. Phillips." I felt relieved because he was smiling.

When I entered Mr. Phillips's office, I noticed several boxes stacked neatly in a corner, and most of the walls were bare.

"Are you changing offices, Mr. Phillips?"

"Well, you could say that, Tyler. I'm actually moving to the Fern Crest Middle school as the new principal."

"Are you for real?"

"I sure am. I guess we'll be seeing more of each other over the next few years."

"Oh, that's great news, Mr. Phillips. Congratulations!"

"Thank you, Tyler! Do you know why I called you to my office?"

"No, not really."

"I have watched the positive changes you have made over the last month, and I want you to be part of my RAK Squad at the middle school."

"The RAK Squad?"

"Yes, it's going to be a student leadership club, and the main focus will be spreading random acts of kindness both in and out of the school. If you accept today, you'll be considered one of its founding members."

"Are you sure you want me to be part of this squad? I've spent most of my time at Fern Creek being a bully."

"That's exactly why I want you to be on this squad. You know the positive impact of kindness. Am I right?"

"Yes, I do," I answered.

"So, are you ready to say yes to being on the RAK squad?" he asked.

"Uhm, yeah, I mean, yes. Thank you, Mr. Phillips."

"It's my pleasure, Ty. Can you think of anyone else who might be a great pick for this team?" Mr. Phillips asked.

"I think Ella, in Mr. Bailey's class, should be on the squad."

"Interesting. I thought your first picks would be Miguel and Cameron. May I ask you why you named Ella?"

"Well, even though I don't know her that well, I watched her encourage R.J., I mean

Preston, during the kickball game. She had the whole class cheering for him, and I think someone like that can be an asset to the squad."

"I think Ella is an excellent choice, Ty. Can you think of anyone else?" asked Mr. Phillips.

"Hmm, I'm sure I can think of a few more students before the end of the day."

"No rush. Think about it and give me four or five more names by tomorrow night," he said.

"Tomorrow night? I'm confused."

"Oh, that's right. You probably haven't heard the news yet. Ella and Mrs. Grant should be telling Mr. Bailey's class right about now. With the help of some well-connected individuals, Ella arranged for the New York Symphony Orchestra to fly in this evening for a special concert tomorrow night at the Portland Theater featuring our very own Preston, recently known as R.J., on the cello! And the whole school is invited!"

"Wow, that's incredible. Ella did that? That's pretty amazing!"

"It sure is! Preston is a music genius, and I can't wait to hear him play. Would you like to help?"

"Help? I can't play an instrument, so I'm not sure I can be a great help."

"I'm pretty sure the New York Symphony Orchestra has that part covered. How would you like to help me pass out programs?" Mr. Phillips asked.

"Yes! Count me in. After all I've done to Preston this year, this will be a great way to make it up to him."

"Great! I'll give your mom a call, and we'll make it happen. I knew I could count on you, Tyler Miller! Now get back to class and enjoy the last day of school. And grab a RAK squad t-shirt from the table as you leave."

"Sure. Okay. Thanks, Mr. Phillips." I grabbed a t-shirt and made my way back to class.

Before entering the classroom, I stopped to read the quote outside Mrs. Granger's door for the last time. "Courage is fire, and bullying is smoke." I still wonder why Mrs. Granger chose this quote above all the others, but I'm glad she did. It sort of describes my life during the last school year. When I let hurt and disappointment guide my decisions, I was blinded by the smokescreen they created. My actions became selfish and hurtful toward others, but I couldn't see it for myself. If I'm being honest, I didn't want to see it.

Fire purifies and makes us stronger, but smoke can blind and confuse us. It takes a lot of courage to step past the smoke and see things for how they truly are. When you're in the smoke, you convince yourself there's no way out. If you do not like who you've become, you can choose to change. It's never too late. I'm thankful for the people that helped me find my courage. It wasn't easy because no matter how often they said it, I refused for a long time to believe what I had become—a bully. Now I can see more clearly.

Hopefully, my parents will work out their problems, and we can be a family again. But, as much as I hate to admit it, there's still a chance nothing will change with them. However, I know I can change my actions and words and let kindness be my guide. With the help of some caring people who believe in me, I am confident I can do it.

A NIGHT TO REMEMBER

THE PORTLAND THEATER WAS bustling with excitement when Tyler entered the stage door and waited for Mr. Phillips to arrive. The backstage pass Mr. Phillips had given him worked like a dream. The security guard let him in without a single question. Tyler couldn't help feeling important as he imagined all the famous people who had already walked through these doors. The backstage area was more interesting than Tyler had imagined. There were pulleys, lights, levers, changing spaces, backdrops, and an overhead catwalk that ran from one side of the performance stage to the other. He tried to take in everything he was seeing.

Ty heard the orchestra warming up. The discordance from all the instruments was the perfect background for the organized mayhem that was going on backstage as the stagehands, lighting technicians, and a man Ty guessed was the production director completed last minute adjustments and preparations for the evening performance.

This was the coolest thing Ty had ever experienced in his life. He wore his best outfit and made sure every hair was in place. From where Ty stood, he could see Preston sitting just a few feet from center stage. It was apparent that Preston was comfortable in these surroundings. Although he was the youngest musician in the group, Preston looked confident and relaxed.

Ty saw the conductor step behind the podium. The stage grew quiet as all the musicians took their stance. Tyler wasn't sure what was happening since it was not time for the concert yet. Suddenly, the conductor began moving his baton through the air, and the room filled with the most glorious sounds within seconds. Ty listened in awe as Preston played his solo. It was as if the music came from his heart. Glancing across the backstage area, Ty noticed that all movement had come to a standstill. No matter how important their job, every person had stopped to listen. For the next ten minutes, the entire room stood mesmerized.

When the last note was played, the room remained silent. The conductor didn't move, nor did anyone else. Ty wanted to applaud with all his might, but the eerie silence paralyzed him. Then the conductor raised his bowed head, turned toward Preston, and began to applaud. Instantly, a roar of applause came from every player, stagehand, and onlooker. Ty gladly joined in with all the gusto he could muster but was startled by an unexpected tap on the shoulder.

"Hey, Ty!" said Ella, surprised to see him backstage.

"Hi, Ella! I didn't expect to see you here," he responded.

Ty was curious about why Mrs. Grant, Mr. Bailey, and two other people he did not recognize were with Ella.

"Well, I'm just as surprised to see you here! Of course, you know Mr. Bailey and Mrs. Grant. This is Marshal Stevens from the Witness Protection Program. He worked with Preston's family getting them settled here in Portland. And this is Mrs. Monahan, my neighbor and a great help in making this surprise for Preston happen. Mrs. Monahan and Marshal Stevens, this is Tyler Miller, a fifth grader at Fern Creek Elementary. Ty, do you know if there's a chair nearby for Mrs. Monahan? Her shoe heel broke as we were walking in, and she twisted her ankle," Ella explained.

Fortunately, Ty knew precisely where to find a stack of chairs. In seconds, he was back with a chair in tow and quickly unfolded it for Mrs. Monahan.

"Thank you, young man!" Mrs. Monahan said as she carefully lowered herself onto the seat. "I should have known better than to wear high heels after nearly a decade of not wearing them. Ella dear, I think you, Mrs. Grant, Mr. Bailey, and Marshal Stevens will have to carry out the surprise without me. Besides I only provided the contacts. If it wasn't for your family and Marshal Stevens, this night would not be happening. The credit belongs to you."

"But, Mrs. Monahan—"

"No, I will not hear of it! Get going now. Time is moving on!" interrupted Mrs. Monahan. "Anyway, I've already had a chat with Preston."

"You did? When?" Ella asked.

"Never you mind, young lady. Be on your way now. After all, this kind young man will look after me," she said, giving Ty a wink.

"Uhm, yes, you can count on me," Ty answered.

The four individuals headed onto the stage. Ty didn't know what was happening. Marshal Stevens was carrying a big case, which was probably another surprise for Preston. Ty watched and listened as Ella made a short speech to Preston, stumbling over an odd sounding word. Preston's puzzled look turned into a happy expression, followed quickly by a shocked one. Ty still wasn't sure what was happening.

Mrs. Monahan, noticing Ty's confused expression, said, "Tyler, Preston is being presented with a very special cello. It's a valuable and extraordinary Man Claudiu cello hand-crafted by Italian artisans. Preston's a truly talented young man who will make beautiful music with that cello!"

"Yes, he is amazing. I have never heard anyone play an instrument the way he plays that cello. I had no idea."

"That's why people are so intriguing to me. I've studied people from all over the world, and there's one thing I know to be true—each individual possesses a degree of genius. The sad truth is that not everyone takes the time to explore their genius. The world would be a better place if we did. Maybe someday it will happen. Promise me that you'll explore your genius, young man." Mrs. Monahan grabbed Ty's hand and waited for him to respond.

After several seconds, Ty lowered his head and asked, "Do you really think I have a genius?"

"You're here, aren't you? There's more to you than you realize. Your life is just beginning. Be willing to learn and grow and always let kindness steer your journey. After all, kindness is the catalyst for opening doors of opportunity."

"Thank you, Mrs. Monahan," Ty said.

"You're very welcome, Tyler."

As the two continued chatting, Mr. Phillips entered backstage with two boxes of programs.

"Ty, are you ready to begin handing out programs?" Mr. Phillips asked.

"Yes, I'm ready, Mr. Phillips! Enjoy the concert, Mrs. Monahan. It was nice to meet you," Ty said as he followed Mr. Phillips toward the door that led into the performance hall.

"It's going to be a wonderful concert! Families are lined up outside the box office and waiting to enter. We better hurry to our places with these programs!" Mr. Phillips said.

***

The next thirty minutes flew by as Mr. Phillips and Ty handed out programs to families from Fern Creek Elementary. As the next hour approached, the theater lights flashed several times, indicating the performance was about to start. As the room lights began to dim, the stage lights illuminated the stage. Music filled the room as the curtain rose, revealing the musicians dressed in the finest attire. They played a good mix of familiar classical pieces for adults and Disney favorites for the students. Each performance ended with rousing applause, and when Preston played "Bach Cello Suite No. 1 in G Major," the audience rose to their feet as he played the final note.

Ty stood in the aisle as Preston rose to receive applause. He held both thumbs in the air and waited for Preston to glance in his direction. As Preston took his bows and scanned the standing audience, he spotted Tyler mid-aisle in the orchestra section, holding both thumbs in the air. For a few seconds, Preston stopped and locked in on Ty and his grand gesture. Kindness prevailed, and the two boys knew it without exchanging words. Giving Ty a quick downward nod, Preston continued scanning the audience and bowing.

Once the applause died down, Preston had a surprise of his own. He introduced Ella, who came on the stage. Preston said she would perform a song with the orchestra accompanying her. When Ella approached the microphone, she looked as confident as Preston had during his performance. Ty had no idea that Ella could sing. He listened in awe. Ty saw a different girl standing on that stage than the withdrawn girl he had seen when he first arrived at Fern Creek Elementary. Ella had changed as much as he had. She was happier and braver. And then it hit him. Maybe he wasn't the only one who allowed kindness to make a positive change. Perhaps, kindness is a more powerful quality than most will ever realize. And someday, he thought as he waited for the applause to subside, he would find the courage to ask Ella and Preston how kindness changed them for the better.

When Ella took her final bow, Preston came and stood beside her. Within seconds the applause started again, and every person—audience, orchestra member, stage hand, lighting director, and backstage crew—was up on their feet. It was a memorable evening. One no Fern Creek student would soon forget.

As the theater began to empty, Ty was joined by his parents, who were seated in the balcony section. Mr. Phillips was joined by his wife, and the five of them decided to end an already fantastic evening with a treat from Fifty Licks Ice Cream, one of Portland's finest. Things were looking up for Ty, but no matter what the future held for his family, he knew the days ahead would be brighter now that he had stepped out of the smoke. It was time to find his genius and make a positive change in the world.

Three Years Later

FERN CREST MIDDLE SCHOOL

THE AUDITORIUM AT FERN Crest Middle School began filling with proud parents and extended family members of its eighth grade students. After three years of hard work, new experiences, and the challenges of becoming teenagers, the students were ready to move on to high school. Some would continue together at Forest Ridge High, while others would venture off to Cypress Creek High School. The Moving Up ceremony would be the last event for these eighth graders before starting their long-awaited summer break.

Mr. Phillips glanced up at the clock on his wall. Realizing that he had twenty-five minutes before the ceremony began, he pulled out his speech for one last review. This group of eighth graders was extra special to Mr. Phillips because they moved with him from Fern Creek Elementary as sixth graders during his first year as principal. He wanted his last words to them to be meaningful and inspiring, just like the RAK Initiative. Just as he was scanning the final paragraph, Mr. Phillips was interrupted by a knock at his door. Looking up, he was glad to see Ella and Tyler.

"Excuse us, Mr. Phillips," Tyler said as he and Ella entered the office.

"Well, look at you two—all dressed up and ready to take on high school. I'm glad you thought to stop by before the ceremony."

"You can always count on us, Mr. Phillips," Ella added, wearing a warm smile.

"How can we help you, Mr. Phillips?" asked Tyler, who was now Mr. Phillip's height.

"Well, today, I don't need your help. Rather, I would like to thank the two of you before the ceremony for the outstanding work you've accomplished with the RAK Initiative. When Mr. Bailey and I started the RAK Initiative six years ago, we hoped to see kindness spread throughout our schools. With your help, the RAK Initiative is now in eight elementary and four middle schools, and several more want to join in the next school year. I can't wait to see what the two of you will do to spread kindness in high school."

"Thank you, Mr. Phillips! Honestly, your belief in me during my time at Fern Creek Elementary still inspires me to spread kindness every day," said Tyler.

"Thank you, Tyler. It was easy to believe in you," Mr. Phillips said.

"Easy? Somehow I don't think that's how I would describe it," chimed Ella, giving Tyler a playful elbow nudge.

"Well, in this case, you're wrong, Ella. Tyler, do you remember the day I told you I was a bully when I was a teenager?" asked Mr. Phillips.

"Yeah, I don't think I will ever forget that day."

"Good. As hard as it is to admit that truth about my past, I'm happy to share it if it can change someone's path for the better. The morning I met you, I could see the old me in you. And—"

"—that's why it was easy to believe in him!" interrupted Ella.

"Exactly, Ella. If I could change for the better, then so could Tyler or anyone else for that matter," Mr. Phillips added.

"Aww, thanks for believing in me, Mr. Phillips," Tyler said.

"And Ella—"

"Yes, Mr. Phillips."

"You have definitely found your purpose, young lady. It's been an honor to be your principal and watch you soar. And that voice of yours truly is a gift. Don't stop singing!"

"I won't, Mr. Phillips. Thank you for your kind words."

"Of course! By the way, have you two ever heard from Preston?" asked Mr. Phillips, hoping for some news.

"No, not directly," Ella said.

"He's been busy flying from state to state playing the cello. And last month he was in Austria and France. He has a huge following on YouTube, me included," said Tyler.

"Yeah, my sister Natalia and I listen to his recorded performances. Hopefully, we can see him live in concert again someday," added Ella.

"Interesting. Did you know that Preston led his school's soccer team to its first championship this year?" asked Mr. Phillips.

"No way! Are you for real?" asked Tyler.

"I sure am. Check out Preston's school's webpage," said Mr. Phillips, facing his laptop toward Ella and Tyler.

"Wow, I'm speechless," said Ella, still in awe of the news.

"When asked how Preston learned to play so well, the article writer states, and I quote, 'I owe my skills to a girl who taught me to play kickball in fifth grade. Even though I couldn't kick the ball to save my life, she never gave up on me. Her kindness and determination opened a new world of possibilities, and I'm forever grateful.'"

"Woah, Ella, Preston is talking about you! That's amazing," said Tyler, giving Ella a fist bump.

The three were interrupted by a knock at the door. Mr. Dobbins, the Assistant Principal, didn't want Mr. Phillips to be late for the ceremony. "It's time, Mr. Phillips," he said, giving Ella and Tyler a thumbs up before heading back to the auditorium.

"Yep. We've got three minutes to get on

stage," said Mr. Phillips, closing his laptop and grabbing the folder holding his speech and announcements. The three walked briskly to the auditorium and found their places just before the ceremony began.

***

The ceremony went smoothly and as planned. Of course, Mr. Phillips was a natural in front of a crowd, and since his words came from the heart, he never once looked down at his prepared speech. Tyler couldn't help feeling happy and a bit proud when he heard Mr. Phillips expressing his confidence in this group of eighth graders to continue spreading random acts of kindness in their next stage of life. Tyler scanned the group of students who had surprisingly become close friends over the last few years—Ella, Thomas, Blake, Andy, Jennilee, Sophie, Laynie, Simon, and even Maddy. The three amigos were tighter than ever and a positive force in their school community.

Tyler considered all that had changed since his challenging fifth grade year and was so grateful. His life's path could have been far different than where it was heading today. He had experienced firsthand the positives in his life from the ripples of kindness, both received and given—and that's often the best life lesson anyone can receive.

ABOUT THE AUTHOR

SINCE 1989, FRANK SARACO has been in the field of elementary education, first as a teacher, then as assistant principal, and currently as principal. Over the years, Frank has learned to relate well with students of different ages, listening to their hopes and dreams and offering genuine support along the way. His natural storytelling ability captivated students, and he dreamed of someday becoming a published author. In 2018, that dream became a reality with the release of his first book, *The Bald and the Beautiful.*

Today Frank pens stories for children, masterfully connecting words to capture curiosity and ignite the creativity inherent in all children. While he writes in different genres, his books are always filled with wonderfully relatable characters that help children explore the possibilities and lessons hidden in their everyday world. From mystery-solving mice to real-world situations, Frank tackles every storyline with believable dialogue and an array of emotions that will speak to every reader, both young and older. His stories spark imagination and take readers on a journey of hope, exploration, and growth and tackle fears encountered by many. This book is Frank's seventh book and the final book in the RAK Initiative Trilogy.

Dear Reader,

If you have a few minutes, please consider leaving a review for this book wherever you purchased it. Reviews help books get found by new readers and are life blood for every author! I'd be so appreciative of your review.

— *Frank Saraco*

Please visit

www.franksaraco.com

to learn about Frank's other books.

www.ingramcontent.com/pod-product-compliance
Lightning Source LLC
Chambersburg PA
CBHW021825090726
47818CB00077BA/49